Let All the Earth

A Contemplative Journey in the North Woods

Albin M. Urbanski

NEPPERHAN PRESS, LLC
YONKERS, NY

Published by Nepperhan Press, LLC
P.O. Box 1448, Yonkers, NY 10702
nepperhan@optonline.net
nepperhan.com

Printed in the United States of America

Library of Congress Control Number: 2010935980

ISBN 978-0-9829904-0-7

Cover art was provided by the author.

DEDICATION

Our Lady of Mount Carmel and my family.

ACKNOWLEDGMENTS

Elizabeth Pinegar, who did the initial editing and was an inspiration.

Fr. Denis Read, O.C.D., who took a beneficent interest.

"Let all the earth cry out with joy to the Lord."

Psalm 66

PREFACE

THERE WAS NO especially clear idea, no awesome moment of awareness, no stunning concept, no careful plan, to write *Let All the Earth*. It just happened.

Of course, it is the result of a great interest in the natural world and the gentle driving movement toward contemplation and contemplative prayer. The interest in how the natural world reflects God did not immediately occur. It perhaps was born long before visiting the "field" as a boy living in an older residential neighborhood of Chicago. The field was an empty lot a few blocks from home, overgrown with weeds, into which my friends and I could burrow, build forts, and imagine ourselves in amazing adventures, and the field became the setting for these adventures, even becoming, though filled with tall weeds, the north woods, mountains, everglades, and whatever our rather fertile imaginations made it. And the field was rich, small as it was, in flora and fauna, to which we paid increasing attention. We began to see.

The deeper understanding of contemplation was born of the philosophers, particularly the ancients, and the development of contemplation to its ultimate is from the Christian contemplatives, especially the Discalced Carmelites. This occurred much later, but somehow I sense the seeds of the contemplative in the field, and even before. Because later, living in the north woods, I began to write about the things we saw, because they were so beautiful, both in themselves and in their interactions. This naturally led to the contemplation of the general idea of the transcendent, which was growing in the field, and from there to God.

The distance from the field appears great, in time and miles, yet it is not so great. It is a moment's time from the boys adventuring in the field to the north woods, from dreams of heroic deeds to openness to God. It is less than a moment's time for the awareness of the Creator, both in the weed banked field and the north woods, in a Church, and in fact anywhere. It is so because of the connection of the natural law to seeing our need to see, as well as the connection of the natural law to reason and language, all being of theological origin. And the desire to see the world around us, to contemplate, leads ultimately to God, if we are only open.

It is not necessary to return to the field, for the field has become the world, and that simply gives us more to contemplate and leads to the ultimate Contemplation. And this was not done by the author alone—the initiative came from elsewhere, from beyond the boys who laughed and imagined in the field, from even beyond the north woods, and all the family and friends and people who had an effect and stirred the seeds, and far beyond the acceptance of contemplative openness—it was from the perfect Humility and superabundant, unconditional Love.

AUTUMN

BY THE RIVER there is a little cove that flows along our land in the north woods where we've mowed the weeds down to a pleasant little spot from which to enjoy the view. Alongside the cove, on either side of it, are bulrushes and a few lily pads. In the evenings the water bugs dance and mark the surface like disappearing pencil marks, and make minute ripples that last for just a moment and are swallowed by the still water.

Occasionally, a fish will roll on the surface of the cove, probably eating the water insects. But there are always many insects on the water in this protected spot. The water soon calms and the insects write on it until dark when you can't see what is on the black, still surface, and the fish roll after them.

A few evenings ago while I stood several feet back from the shoreline, a bat whizzed past me and made a graceful series of banks and turns, gently dimpling the surface of the calm water while eating the bugs on it. The display of flying was amazing and wonderful. Swallows are like that too. And the larger, more graceful night hawks. The bat put on a fine aerobatic display, then was gone. Across the river against the darkening sky, other bats turned and dived, pursuing relentlessly and beneficially unseen flying insects. The bats flicked against the remaining light, and I watched until I could only see an occasional flash of bat against the dark sky.

In the cove a beaver swam quietly, almost gliding along the water, only his upper head and part of his back visible. He slid into the bulrushes and disappeared. Soon he returned, nibbling a twig or plant of some sort, and when he saw me, slipped noiselessly under water in a complex-looking swirl, the only visible thing by now.

There is an order here. Not unfathomable, but sometimes hidden. Hidden by too much of a culture's superficiality, and hidden by a fear of looking deeply at why we are, and where we are from.

The question, for instance, of creation must arise. And from that, the study of it for thousands of years and the logical thrust and drive, comes really only one answer. And what an answer. This order in which and of which we live comes from the ultimate of Order. The order includes us, we also are a part of nature, and we do use nature. Certainly nature can destroy us, but it wouldn't know it. We call the ultimate Order that knows, God. And it is more, too, more than Order. But what a place to begin.

Sometimes the order of the cove is frightening. The shriek of a rabbit caught by an owl, frogs trapped by raccoons standing in the water. Even the insect battles. Yet there is an order and a purpose. We do learn from nature because we, our bodies and souls, are part of created being. They tell us part of what we are, they are not simply our "possession," but part of creation. That order. From higher Order. From God.

The cove elicits metaphysics from many people because it's there. Like we are. The beauty of the cove is sometimes ignored, or passed over casually, or hidden, or forgotten. But it is surely there. Some people might say it is not beautiful. I have not heard that. Of course, no one can say it is totally inconsequential. If the cove were to disappear, it would not perhaps have a lasting effect as if a human disappeared. But an effect would have been lost or changed.

The trees across the river from the cove reflect the mystery and present a mysterious stage. They reflect in the river, especially on very calm mornings and evenings when the current is invisible. They tease the imagination to portray what lies only a few feet within them. Perhaps they offer what explorers have always reacted to—a sense of seeing what is ahead, or beyond—a curiosity perhaps of what has been and is not now seen. A desire for awareness. Mankind has that desire to know. And it's not just a biological reaction or instinct. Rather, it appears to be a matter of choice based on a series of alternatives. It is an essential and intellectual thing, rather than strictly a bio-pathological one.

Those trees across the river are especially lovely in the fall in the way the river reflects their colors. The colors appear to constantly change almost imperceptibly, but really with the actuality of the clock, until the winter peels the last leaves from the baring branches. They look thin and ghostly in the night, particularly the white birches, yet they still look lovely. Still majestic, like all the things of nature are majestic, although the prey and preyed upon, still not quite understood, can baffle, unless one finds the key in fallenness, in incompleteness. But that always reminds one that man's things are majestic too, even in their fallenness and incompleteness, if they move toward the fullness of truth.

Colonnades in buildings and the variety of architecture are amazing. They reflect nature like the river in another way. They reflect the ambience of order, not the individual tree, or area, or relationships. They reflect a balance and harmony which does exist in the seemingly haphazard. The order is so massive we sometimes miss it. We see one pine needle and miss its significance in the order of countless pine needles. We see no order in a dozen pine needles, but they fit into an ordered pattern when complemented by the pine trees and by other types of leaves.

The art which has survived, which passed the test of time, reflects order as well as manifesting a special perception. The artist, whether poet, musician, painter, or sculptor, perceives in a special way, and places his perception into the vehicle of his art, the technical expertise, the concrete element. The development of that art depends on apperception, the amalgamation of countless experiences relevant to that moment's conception, and then the artist works in the concrete, technical expertise of the particular art form. The act, the art of creation of all things, the First Cause, does it another way—with total love.

The stag horn sumac are turning their bright and deep, almost rust, red color. It seems to have happened overnight. Yesterday there was barely a hint of change in their leaves, this morning they are almost fully red, fully colored.

The ferns in the low places have been touched by frost and are weathering. They are so delicate looking, yet so very tough, that it is almost surprising that a mild frost affects them. They are always a pleasure to see popping up quickly in the spring, but that is a long way from now.

Now they are brown and wrinkled from the frost, although in sheltered places fresh bright green ones still grow and bow their delicate fingers in soft arcs over the ground. They are like dancers clustered on stage in a collective yet individual grace, a harmony of growth and life.

But the sumacs above the ferns are brightening, and the red they turn is so deep that when the sun strikes them fully, they appear acrylic painted. In dying they brighten. Their leaves are long and slim and graceful, and are now turning from deep green to dark poinsettia crimson. The branches and stalks, when bare and visible, immediately hint at their popular name, "stag horn," with a little imagination, of course.

The flowers still bloom. Rather, some of the flowers still bloom, the ones whose essence guides them to flower in the fall, "the force that through the green fuse drives," for reasons unknown to us, delight in color and form.

Among the most striking is the Closed Gentian with its very blue five towers. I saw it first among tall weeds, alone but very visible, tucked into them. The flower is an intense blue, bluer than the sky, bluer than deep lakes and oceans. Perhaps a different blue, too, and recently I've seen more blooming among the tall weeds. They almost hide, then when near, express their previously surreptitious glow to the visitor. But how many have never been seen? Their existence provides a reflection then of immense and ineluctable beauty.

Wonder and awe are partners in a true awareness of beauty. Truth is beauty, beauty truth, said the philosophers, and reality is not relative, but exists outside the mind. The source of beauty is not the mutable, but rather He that loves superabundantly.

There are many flowers that I haven't identified yet, but they are there to be enjoyed—their colors, their shapes, their perfume. The tiny blue, yellow, and white flowers my mother called "baby blue eyes" bloom all year at the edge of the cove. The buttercups are everywhere; their gold stands out against the green of others. And the scent of flowers is often gently constant in the air, wafting in the breeze in differing and teasing intensity.

In the fall, the smell of the air varies, as it does in other seasons, but there is a distinct smell to the woods in autumn. On wet or foggy days the smell of damp wood pervades the area mixed with the smell of wet earth and vegetation. The pleasantly acrid terebinth-like smell. It is distinctly north woods. It is especially north woods autumn when the leaves and pine needles are coming down and are either soaked by the rains or dried to a dusty ground coating. The wet leaves are silent for walking, except for the occasional dry one that has somehow avoided the "wet." But one can walk almost noiselessly through the wet woods, as can the deer and other animals.

In dry times the coating of leaves on the ground prevents any silent movement, and even the deer crunch through the woods, although more silently than I. And always at this season is the dusty dry or woody wet smell of leaves and woods.

Now that the leaves have begun falling, it is possible to see longer distances through the woods, as though a veil were lifted and exposed a private place, a secret hideaway. There is much to see too, if you look carefully: the rocks jutting up and lichen and mosses still holding on to them, and the many trees. The varieties of brush and flowers and tiny saplings of potentially great trees, the trunks, each different, of tall red and white pines, and spruce, balsam, cedars, and the deciduous trees like oaks, cherry, basswood, and maples with their pointed colors. There are many more. The ghostly white birch and gray brown aspen lie rotting where they fall, providing for other plants and animals.

The first look one takes into this mysterious bower, one sees confusing things—a jumble of branches, twigs, leaves, needles, stumps, trunks—angled, straight, bent, curved, bowed, and colors of every shade and blend. Subsequent looks gradually find order and patterns and reasons, yet everything remains. An embodied fascination.

Two tiny flying squirrels surprise me in the early evening, squirting down a pine and across the path, scattering the dry leaves. They are playful and quick, chasing each other about, occasionally feeding, and late at night moving from tree to tree during their active time. Sometimes they will glide to the ground from a tree. I have seen it only once, the not believable sight of a squirrel in a sort of a very controlled fall from a tree. It appears to be a means of escape, but perhaps I simply haven't been out at night enough or visually keen enough in the dark to see them.

The squirrels are active and appear playful. They are, of course, very alert, since they are food for several types of predators. Although the flying squirrels are quite safe in trees, except perhaps for the Pine Marten which is capable of catching them up there, they are also susceptible to being caught on the ground by predators like the fox.

I saw a beautiful fox this morning while I was walking on the road. It was a tawny gold color and was hunting mice along the edge of the gravel driveway. I've never seen a fox such a light golden color. The white tip on the tail was visible, but not as contrasting as on some foxes. We had one near the house some years back which had a black tail. It was beautiful—a deep red coat and the black tail with a bright white tip. And as the fox trotted along, the black tail would lean straight back like a banner.

Last week, early in the morning, a fox was resting in the weeds behind the house. It was lying down, though very alert, its ears constantly flicking from side to side, often not synchronically. After resting and looking about with its ears straight up and constantly turning, it finally rose and trotted down the trail to the cove. Probably had a mouse breakfast. It seemed quite relaxed for all its alertness.

The fantastic fox has appeared again. This time crossing the lawn from the woods on one side to the woods on the other. His (or her) fur looks freshly brushed and almost gleams in its richness, its golden tan color. The tail was held straight out as seems usually to be the case. We hope to see it prancing about more often. It almost seems to be aware of how beautiful it is, having a kind of casual superiority in its movements. Of course, that's only personifying. If no one saw it, it would still be beautiful, still reflect beauty, grace, and order.

We hope diligently that the fox will not be trapped. The monetary return seems irrelevant to the beauty of the furry fox, and even if no one saw it, there should be, it seems, a rather strong reason for not killing the thing. We are to be stewards of nature, not slaughterers, yet there is an atavistic philosophical reason for "catching" something, for having it, despite the beauty of the fox alive. Some may see more monetary value in it than other value, but that ignores something vital.

The sun in autumn is often softened by the haze and fog that seems so prevalent at that time of the year. The mornings are often foggy, usually due to the warm ground or water in contact with the cooler air of night. "Convection fog" is the appropriate term. This fog is simply a chemical reaction, a molecular occurrence, but in the woods, and on the river, it is magic. The beginnings of convection fog on the river, the little whispers of smoke rising from the water as the sun sets, are sometimes called "ghost's breath."

The sun came up this morning over the autumn haze as a blood red ball, a huge light, stained molten red, first peeking an eye over the haze line, then flowing upward, slowly higher until only the bottom fraction of an arc was hidden. As it rose it brightened, losing the liquid burning red fire image and becoming supernova bright, as a sun should apparently be.

It was an autumn sunrise and stopped me in awe. What art we are privy to see, to be a part of. What great things we can see. Can they really have just occurred? There is too much order, there is too much variety, there is too much ineluctable existence to not accept the Great Creator, a supreme artist of inestimable awe, who paints in a medium no one else can, and for, at least in some sense, us. We must see, contemplate, to gain a foothold to the truly transcendent. This is part of, and for, in infinite ways, us.

Sometimes we seem to separate mankind from the rest of nature—the hills and forests and mountains and oceans, and everything else. Human beings too are certainly part of nature. Above it in one sense, but still part of it. A most complex and beautiful part, reflecting more than all the rest, the image of Creator.

The sun doesn't in itself initiate such thoughts, its relationship to everything else does. When the sun set yesterday, a group of Canada geese decided to rest at our cove. They settled in by dark with a gentle chuckling and clucking. A purely biological act, apparently, with cause and effect in the setting sun and physiological needs triggered by light factors. But they came in, in order, a certain order, and there was a momentary poem in the air.

This morning the mowed grass by the cove was full of their droppings. A bit ungracious, I thought initially, but certainly not unnatural. The purely biological perhaps—not poetic a bit.

The geese are bunching together in small flocks, as are the ducks, and it won't be long before they start moving south. A dozen Canada geese passed low over the river this morning looking like planes buzzing the water. They "honked" occasionally and sped by in a straight line about four feet above the surface. An exciting look, buzzing the river. Later in the day five ducks, probably mallards, in a rough diamond formation with one trailer, swept toward the house, and when within 50 feet banked east and climbed rapidly until they disappeared beyond the pines. They held perfect formation on each other, and congratulated themselves with an occasional gentle quack as they flew by.

The deer have almost completely lost their reddish summer coats and have put on their winter gray. One doe that frequents our yard with her twin fawns was gray weeks ago. Her twins still have a reddish tinge to their coats, but they still also have some remnants of their fawn spots. Another doe that we often see also has a set of twins. These are much larger than the former's. The younger-looking twins must have been born in late June, while the older set probably early May.

On one occasion we saw both mothers and both sets of twins in different parts of the yard at the same time. It was rather nice. We've also had a couple of bucks around; one "spike" buck, which feeds on our lawn fearlessly up to the house, and a more reticent four-pointer. They are both regular visitors; they are, however, boorishly eating our cedar ornamentals in front of the house.

We have also seen many very large tracks in the sand by the driveway. One of these days we'll see that deer itself. I suspect it will be a beauty. We are hoping the spike buck that visits our yard often will survive the upcoming deer-hunting season. He is a bit casual about us being around, and only looks up when we pull the car out of the garage. Perhaps he will become a bit more wary when there are more people in the woods shooting.

While walking down the drive and watching the ground for tracks, I heard a noise behind me, turned, and was pleasantly surprised to see two rather large porcupines stroll somewhat haughtily across the drive. The first one walked straight ahead and ignored me, but the second deigned to glance in my direction. Naturally, I greeted him or her, and he or she stopped immediately and erected its quills, looking at me in a distressed manner. After a few minutes it strolled off in an ungainly way, the quills still erect. They were both about 15 or 20 pounds, and were humorous-looking as they almost waddled along. That was the second time in a couple of months that I saw a porcupine on our driveway, which by the way is about a half-mile long, and whose sandy sides are a great signpost of animals who visit.

The porcupine has been called a "starving" (or "lost") man's supper, since it is slow and easy to catch, and probably can be killed by striking it in the head. Porcupines do not "shoot" their quills, although they may slap their tails at someone or something harassing them. The tails are, or course, full of sharp quills, and many of them are loose enough to easily strike and stick in the "harasser." The quills themselves have tiny barbs on the sharp end, the better to hold fast when they puncture. The barbs are easily visible under a low-power microscope or even a good magnifying glass.

The porcupine has been around tens of thousands (or more) of years and doesn't really cause much harm. Some claim that it destroys trees. Yes, it sometimes girdles the trees by stripping the bark around them, but usually it only rips some bark off or eats the buds. It eats twigs and other forms of arboreal vegetation also, but hardly is a destroyer of forests. It is an unusual and interesting animal with its pointed defense.

The sun was warm today, and it was windy and clear after last night's frost, the first heavy one of the year. Close to the river along the trail I flushed two ruffed grouse, the first I've seen in this area. They rose out of the brush in a roar of wings as I turned. If I had been hunting them I would have had nothing, since they flew between heavy brush and trees in their even rapid wing beat.

Ruffed grouse are great if you like a challenge in hunting and shooting. They are also good eating. A bit dry, but very tasty. I don't hunt much now but have had some lovely afternoons trudging through the woods after grouse, and looking forward to the burst of flight, and the sound of very rapid wing beats. They are, certainly, easy to miss, which is no problem, because the hunt is primarily to be in the woods.

The ruffed grouse, the spruce grouse (rare in our area), and the sharp-tailed grouse—the latter not as common as the former—

create "booming" sounds during mating, which can occur from spring through summer. The sound is created by rapid wing movements according to ornithologists, and the male usually selects a fallen log or logs from which to boom. This attracts females. It's true. Music hath charms.

The booming starts loudly, and slowly, and settles into almost a slow drum roll sound as it fades off. Another pleasant and interesting sound of the woods, and one that is difficult to pinpoint. The sound is deep and lovely, coming from some mysterious areas of the woods.

A few minutes after the grouse flushed, a great blue heron flew over and settled into the bulrushes along the river. A graceful bird with long legs, long neck, and long beak, the heron strolls and stands patiently in the shallows feeding on a variety of insects, frogs, and small fish. It is a pretty big bird with a wing span of, in a mature bird, up to five feet. They have sort of a lumbering flight, but carry on in an unperturbed way. Once, at dark, while I was standing on a dock in a northern lake watching the northern lights, a heron almost flew into me. I saw his silhouette at the last moment and ducked. The heron saw me, it appears, at the same time, squawked loudly and frantically, yet with some attempt at dignity climbed for altitude over me and flapped away, irritatedly squawking from his fright.

The Canada geese are flying over in smallish groups, gathering for the long flight south. Their "honking" is an exciting sound, reflecting great movement and certainly an uncanny sense of direction. A special kind of direction and order, I think.

Last night the wind was very strong, gusting to about 30 miles per hour, and even in the dark you could see the tops of the pines bending and whipping against the lighter sky.

The sound of the wind through the pines is unique, and with the rustling of leaves in the deciduous trees the wind produces a cacophonous concert, rising and falling and scaling in new and fresh ways. Going to sleep listening to this wind song through the trees is most pleasant and relaxing. It also brings memories of warm beds and a coming winter outdoors. That strong wind shook down acorns from the oaks, particularly from the large oak in our front yard. The deer took advantage of this, as did some squirrels, and by late afternoon the dark gray doe and her twins were browsing under the oak and were within 10 feet of the bedroom windows, behind which we lay and watch.

Later in the evening they were back, as was the spike buck. The adults ignored each other, and the fawns, occasionally leaping and chasing each other, ran in circles around both the doe and the buck, and the buck moved gradually onto the fringes of the acorn area.

Finally, when it was quite dark they began to leave. First the buck, then the doe, and finally the fawns. You could hear the doe calling from the woods in that peculiar coughing-exhaling sound, almost like a bark. Once in a while the fawns would return the coughing sound toward the doe in the woods.

Soon they turned into the woods and sauntered out of sight and by then all you could see clearly was their white tail outlines. The deer spend quite a bit of time in our yard, which isn't terribly large, but it is bounded by the woods in the front where the driveway passes, and in the back the slope toward the river is open for about 50 yards. The deer feed in the weeds and among the sumac quite a bit. The fawns also chase each other about, and play in these open areas. Of course, as mentioned, they do seem to enjoy the acorns.

Today during breakfast we spotted some movement in the sky. It turned out to be a bald eagle, and evidently, from the white head and tail, a mature one. It circled for a while over our part of the river, gradually losing altitude until, in its passing closest to the house, we could define the beak and its gleaming white head and tail feathers. It was probably looking for fish in, or on, the river.

Once I saw an eagle feeding with crows on a car-killed deer, and several times I have seen immature bald eagles (no white feathers) feeding with crows. They, like most wild animals, are opportunists, and have to be, concerning food.

We haven't seen too many eagles this year. They generally work the length of the river, searching for fish, dead or alive, or whatever food is available.

I have seen eagles swoop to the water's surface and pick up fish, and it is an exciting thing to see, but far more exciting is the dive of an osprey, called a "fish eagle" in some areas, to catch a fish.

The osprey soars, looking for fish, and when it discovers a potential target, hovers or banks sharply and dives, sometimes straight down, sometimes folding its wings partly, sometimes spreading them before it hits the water. Quite often the bird will rise and flap away with a fish in its talons.

It is an impressive display and worth watching. One of the wonders around us that we might take in with some sense of awe. Certainly, there are marvelous things that stimulate a feeling of awe, and human relationships do that also. Yet we are so jaded by them we ignore their awesomeness. Sometimes we ignore mankind in our picture of environmental concerns, except as the cause of pollution and other problems.

Man, of course, is certainly also a part of nature, although quite obviously at a level different from the other created elements of what we call nature. But our bodies are not simply our possessions to casually do with as we wish, they are part of "us" also. Within certain bounds, within certain parameters, we function as body and spirit. To go beyond those parameters is to be abusive. Thus, there are things the natural world teaches. For instance, we can derive all sorts of mathematically proven concepts or "laws" from "nature," such as the physical laws. Furthermore, nature teaches us, or we can learn from nature, certain directions. Not simply to replace the transcendent directions of the spiritual, of revelation, but as created things, not totally separate from the transcendent which is a normal part of created being. From that comes the natural law that humankind knows, about which Cicero said that whoever disobeys it is fleeing himself, rejecting human nature, and will suffer the greatest penalties. And humans contemplate. We contemplate because the natural law is written in us, on us, of us.

The glowing bright reds of sumac are now gone. The heavy frosts the last two nights killed the sumac. Most of the leaves curled and fell off, and those remaining on branches are curled and dead.

Sometimes the brightness lasts for a week or so, but this year the two hard frosts in a row eliminated that special brightness. The branches now are bare and do look somewhat like the antlers of a deer. On the ground are slivers of red color, the narrowed bright leaves of the sumac. The wind scatters them further and further, into crevices and among brush and between weeds until they are gone. The brush is prepared for winter. It is entering its dormant state.

The wind in the autumn is not only felt, it is heard. It is also heard in other seasons, but in the late autumn it seems to begin up high in the tallest trees, and swishes and hisses through, bending and swaying them against the sky. Clusters of pine needles and occasional branches fall to the ground.

In the middle heights of the forest the wind whips large tree limbs, wearing them slowly left and right, and roars through the bushes and brush tops clattering branches and twigs against each other. Leaves, more twigs, and seed casings fly to the ground. Low to the ground the wind is softer and smoother, and arcs the tall grasses and weeds and small shrubs to bow down. In bare or sandy spots it throws handfuls of dust which quickly dissipate; seeds and bits of dry weeds flutter before it. And sometimes, when you see a fox stand searching a field for mice, the wind makes whorls in its fur, and the fox stops, raises its nose to the windy sky, and whips its full banner tail to the side.

On the cooling water the wind draws designs and lines and ripples and curls and sometimes white caps. It has its own unseen way. All you can see is its art. It is well organized and is an effect of effects of a cause. It is well organized.

At the river this evening, as the sun had just set and the air suddenly cooled to about 40 degrees, three ducks silhouetted themselves against the brightest part of the clear sky as they flew up river. By now not a breath of air moved, and the river was perfectly calm. A fish rolled in the middle, making a silver line on the black water. The sky directly above me was already a dark blue, and the lighter part in the west receded. Another flight of ducks, five this time, beat quickly up river. One star shines beyond the ducks. Jewel bright, it must be Venus shining as the westering sunlight recedes even more. The woods are very quiet except for an occasional rustle, where a squirrel or mouse moves about. It is already dark, and I cannot see more than 20 or 30 feet into the woods. The smell of pine is rich, and needles litter the trail back to the house, blown there by the recent winds. Stars are blinking on. Soon the sky will be awesomely filled with stars, and the Milky Way will be a wide stroke of brightness across it. There will be no moon tonight. The stars will light the sky alone.

An owl hoots gently across the river. The silence itself is expressive. The sound is closer now. Nothing else makes a sound. It is contemplatively quiet.

In the morning the fog coats the river just as light appears before dawn. It lies softly in slowly rolling mounds. Across the gentle valley to the east, the fog billows quietly through the trees. The weeds in front of the house are pure frost white, and the large field at the end of our drive is gleaming in the rising sun. It is purest silver-white, and each blade of tall grass and tuft of seed on top is painted with it.

The world has turned white, a thin crystalline veneer of such fragility and delicacy that the rising sun makes it disappear without a trace except for a few beads of pure water on the grasses.

The air on such mornings is sharp and clear, and every inhalation a promise of the future day. Its ambience is pregnant with coming occurrences, adventures and calms, activity and rest, the warmth of autumn afternoons and the twilight of fall smells.

The sun continues to warm off the frost until only isolated shady pockets avoid it, retaining their chill coat until eventually they bare themselves like their surroundings.

When the frost was almost gone in the open field, one of our "resident" does and her twin fawns strolled out of the woods to eat fallen acorns under the big oak. They were very relaxed, and the fawns, who have now lost their spots and are as gray as their mother, decided to play and chase each other about. They began by gently butting one another, then rushing in circles, one after the other. At the end of one of these circuits, one of the fawns rushed to its mother and attempted to nurse; the doe stood still for several minutes, and then turned away and trotted a few feet off. It seems she is weaning them slowly.

The spike buck we've seen so often in the backyard appeared in the front and joined the three deer already there in eating acorns. At one point all four deer had their heads down, their front legs spread widely to facilitate reaching the acorns, chewing contentedly. Of course, they soon raised their heads and looked around, and scanned their ears for unusual sounds, then returned to their eating.

They stayed for about 40 minutes and finally moved away into the woods, the twins bursting into play after longer periods of eating.

By then the river had cleared entirely of fog, and the first breaths of wind mottled and wrinkled its surface. Close to the other shore, a fish rolled, the sun just catching the splash and turning it into a spark. A fast flight of mallards, five of them, shot down the center of the river about 10 feet above it. The woods were coming to life, and the chipmunk in the rock garden sat on a rock in a patch of rising sunlight, his eyes half closed, chirping alone in his measured "chuck, chuck" song. Every sound caused a tremor of his whole body, and he looked too serious standing there singing to the warming autumn world.

This evening I decided to walk our drive in the dark, just for the adventure of it. I started as the light in the west was just fading, and the sky was magenta and purple and dark red. As I walked out of the house, a loud high-pitched scream sounded above me, making me start for a moment. Turning quickly, I saw a hawk soaring about 200 feet above the house. It looked like a red-tailed hawk, although it was difficult to identify in the fading light, common in this area, and a very graceful bird. It circled widely and solemnly several times, barely moving its wings as it seemed to be in a thermal, even at this late time of daylight, in a column of rising warm air, screeching every 30 seconds or so. It finally dove gently behind the trees and out of sight.

I have seen a hawk pounce on a mouse or meadow vole in a field, and they have been seen soaring at 1500 feet in the same thermal as a sailplane, circling off a wing tip of the aircraft. On one occasion we had four kittens playing in the backyard when, without warning, a large Cooper's hawk glided over them, its talons outstretched, but at the last instant, only a few feet above the unknowing kittens, it flapped furiously and flew away over the trees. Perhaps the hawk saw me, or decided the kittens were too large.

One of the more amazing hawks is the kestrel, the American kestrel, or sparrow hawk. Slightly larger than a large robin or blue jay, the kestrel often hovers over one spot, beating its wings rapidly, searching for its prey, and then drops almost straight down to strike. Usually its prey consists of large insects like grasshoppers, but occasionally it will take a mouse. They often sit on power lines, or fences in open fields or meadows, and have the typical hawk-shaped head and beak. Very handsome little birds. Gerard Manley Hopkins' great poem, "Windhover," is titled after the European kestrel and is used metaphorically to paint a poem of God's creatures. Complexity and simplicity in one.

The hawk I saw above the house has been staying around the area. Several times he's been sitting at the top of a dead tree next to the drive. Perhaps he can easily see any movement of mice or ground squirrels across the light colored gravel drive. He too is a handsome bird.

Walking along the drive at night is exciting in a certain way. Especially if you stop regularly and remain very still, then you can hear all sorts of sounds in the woods. The rustling of nocturnal mice and flying squirrels, the movement of raccoons and skunks, the raccoons' "chirring" sounds, a weasel darting in the underbrush, deer moving about. If you're fortunate, you might hear a fox bark or "yip," a clear, crisp sound that carries a bit of adventure with it, the owl hooting from across the river, and an answering hoot from the woods behind the house. These are just some sounds identifiable quite readily. Of course, many of the sounds can't specifically be identified, and then imagination comes into play. Sometimes it is overactive. Usually, it just leads to a conclusion of not knowing the sound, especially when the night is windy and the trees sway and branches click and clack, and the sound of the wind through the pines rises and falls in a hissing sigh. The leaves rustle in various tones and octaves, depending on the tree and its size, and overall the wind provides a dark and pleasantly mysterious symphony at night in the woods.

Sometimes the only sound one hears is silence. It is a lack of sound, but only in one sense. There is the silence of God's answer to our supplication, and it too is more than a lack of sound; it is an answer so that we can understand the Word in our limited way.

A heavy wind can be truly frightening, for limbs, some quite large and dangerous to someone below, can come crashing down, and an old dead tree, if weak enough, can fall, smashing everything in its way. Once in a while, on a windy day or night, especially in a summer storm where wind gusts can be quite high, you can hear the crash of an old tree toppled by the force of the wind.

In winter a heavy wind combined with an icy rain, or thick wet snow, can cause trees to topple, and branches to snap and fall. The sound is sharp and loud.

This evening the sky in the west is still bright with the rays of the setting sun, and the woods around me will be dark soon, but now the air itself seems golden. The air itself appears gold colored in these last rays of the sun. The profusion of different shades of gold and yellow, and subtly arranged amber leaves here on the path to the cove, seems to have been extended to the atmosphere. It's as though a brilliant haze has descended on the area. The pines and other evergreens have simply melted into the background. Beyond the house to the north and east there are maples of deep shades of red and rust, almost every one a slightly different shade, and they are all touched by the golden air.

Here by the cove, though, the gold holds a breathless colored secret ambience. Above the gold "layer" is a bright glare of sky; against this blue white sky a lone bat, almost the color of the haze layer, arcs and curves and turns and rolls, catching the remaining fall insects. Most of the bats have already gone south in great masses at night. This ace seems to prefer extending and preserving summer. Now he's gone behind the trees, and then immediately flares vertically into a rapid hammerhead stall, and then down again. Pure silhouette of dance against the bright stage of sky, while the air around the ground burns with the glow of gold autumn.

Sophocles said, "One must wait until the evening to see how splendid the day has been." Although he meant it metaphorically, of course referring to more than the pleasantness of the day itself, it springs to mind that this evening ends appropriately a splendid day.

In the late evening the wind arose again, and in the last glow of day in the west a line of clouds appeared, thin on the horizon. The dead leaves flew off the trees, in some spots making short lived blizzards. Every step crunches leaves, and the falling ones often gently touch your head and shoulders. Sometimes you can extend your hands and catch the falling leaves. It does usually require some dexterity, though, especially when the wind is heavy and gusting.

Later last night the cloud line I saw in the evening rained large drops on the roof, and the wind roared. Distant thunder rumbled behind the wind.

This morning the sky was gray and low, with a cold drizzle hazing everything. The wind remained sharp and heavy, and staying in bed was an especially comfortable thought. Days like this when the pines bend, and the deciduous trees rattle, and the wind is cutting, are days where you fire a wood stove and absorb the warmth while watching winter prepare. There will still be good warm weather, but this nip is a warning of the cold of winter.

These are days to be excited about. The leaves falling from the trees open the woods to view, and besides the innumerable effects that fall has on the environment and the chemical changes that occur, the cold wind and cold rain drops bring an invigoration, which is simply different than the invigoration of every other season.

There is reason for invigoration despite the world news of violence and hate and disingenuousness as a common helping.

This invigoration is not only in the atmospheric pressure and the autumn signs. It is in the hope, faith, and dignity of the transcendent. Those people who ignore that, ignore the ground of hope and faith. As Rabbi Abraham Joshua Herschel says, human dignity comes from the awareness that there is something greater than us. The invigoration we feel on a "special" day is perhaps only the manifestation of a greater thing, and dignity is sibling to faith and hope—not pomposity, or arrogance, but dignity, the great divinely equalizing quality that the "least" humans have.

Sometimes a form of invigoration comes from the biological: the appetite being gratified, or the remembrance of pleasant times, or even high atmospheric pressure and a crisp, cool day. But to speak of invigoration on a higher plane, as in a more sophisticated and complex mode, we have to transcend that which can be defined as biological life and move to "essence." Not just mobility and reproduction, but free will and conceptualization. The essence that makes a thing what it is, as Aristotle called it. One who would ignore this would ignore most of life, would ignore the elements that distinguish.

The invigoration of the spirit can even have an ameliorative effect on the physical; there is indeed connection. And the natural world is not divorced from the spiritual, but is not the same, and we, who are aware of it, have as part of us that spiritual essence which allows us to be aware of the transcendent.

Every day the leaves fall from the trees and open the woods a bit more. Etiolation draws the green from the leaves and the grasses and the ferns, and the woods not only open, they also change color. A heavy rain and/or wind will speed the process. Soon we'll be able to see a wide stretch of the river as it curves by the land. Now, already, small patches of the river appear through the woods along the shore where the leaves have fallen away. The river glimmers through these spaces and glistens when the wind blows them left and right.

The autumn atmosphere is, as it is relevantly so in other seasons, regularly beautiful. This evening it was especially so. After the sun set the moon appeared, a thin crescent in the western sky with Venus glowing above her. A thin faint line of light remained on the horizon, and the clear dark blue, almost blue-black sky, contrasted strongly with the moon's visible graceful sliver.

Not a sound could be heard. The night animals were moving, but not a sound could be heard under that bright crescent of moon.

The animals hunting and moving about in the night seem so separated and foreign to us, but they are also seen in the day occasionally where they are more familiar. Of course, in the day they retain a special recognizable partnership or familiarity in our minds. But the reality is that there is always some connection, although the differences are obviously enormous. The connection becomes tenuous, however, when we begin to discuss awareness and thought.

Still, sometimes we totally separate man from "nature," as though nature were all the natural environment, and mankind somehow intruding upon it. No, mankind is a created element, though a special element with the capability of stewardship. Nature without man is dismembered; without God it is inane. But to paint a picture of the "natural" world and place mankind in it as simply just another part equal to all the others is also to falsify reality. It is, furthermore, an erratic convulsion of logic to ignore the self-evident difference and superiority of mankind over the other elements of nature. But there certainly is a connection in the order, with cause-and-effect relationships. That is why we should be stewards, wise users, in various ways, of nature.

Reason, free will, and conceptualization provide a capability beyond the single elements of "nature," and cannot have produced themselves. There are mysteries, but most of them relate to human insufficiency in relation to the whole of creation. It is absurdity to speak of evolution unless one predicates and sees that such an evolution must be guided and directed; the amoeba can't pull itself to another level by its "bootstraps." And that has to be done by a power necessarily far greater than anything at a visible or knowable level.

Beauty interferes pleasantly with such interesting, and important, ruminations, and is in itself the focus of much intellectual deliberation. Beauty is part of what we must cherish. It is immutable. But let us again mention the sliver of moon, so relentlessly and sharply white hanging on the blueblack sky, and touching very lightly the tops of the trees across the river, so you could tell they were hazy pastel green on black.

On the river the moon was no less bright, only it had the fine wrinkles of the water, which, although still, was fluid, and fluid rich remained.

Fluid richness is not a result of reason, though reason takes us there. It is a result of heart. Blaise Pascal, the brilliant eighteenth century scientist, mathematician, and philosopher agreed that reason and the mind can take humans to a certain point of understanding, and then we must rely on a transcendent faith. Reason does not just drop us simply off into nothingness but takes us to that point and points the way beyond itself; it gives us a direction and rule. It isn't that Pascal's use of reason stopped. It is that reason took him as far as it could, pointed out the truth surrounded in mystery, and bade him use the tools appropriate to that mystery and acceptance of our own inability to be all and understand all, without the aid of the Creator we call God. From Him, the ultimate of perfection, all beauty and reason must come, as well as those ultimate tools and goals, faith, hope, and love. The heart. And love, dying for and before the other, is even greater than reason.

The sliver of moon is behind the trees and will be setting soon. It is as bright as when I first looked at it, perhaps brighter against the now very dark sky, with Venus sharp above it.

Nothing still is heard from the woods or river. Not a wind exists. Everything has stopped for a short time. Soon the owl will call, and the rustling in the woods will begin again. There has been a heavy comma on the night.

St. Francis of Assisi knew perfectly where to punctuate the sentences and paragraphs of his understanding of the relation between the natural environment, man, and God. He reveled in the beauty around him, in the beauty of mankind too, and in the beauty and greatness of God. His love of nature and animals was not some cloying sentimental personification or anthropomorphism, but a real love based on their creation by God. His ability to relate and connect and affect nature around him was a miracle, based on his opening himself to God's will. His love of people was certainly no less great and certainly far more, in the appropriate way, and his love of God, of course, was primary.

St. Francis wasn't just an "environmentalist," he was lover and steward and humble servant. He was this to God, and therefore he was this in all ways.

His compassion was real, not based on imaginary assessments of the things and people around him. His "worldview" was non-self-profiting (nor self-pitying), only one of service, not demeaning mankind or abusing nature, but understanding the priorities in a realistic manner, and committed to the highest priority, God. An idea of serving or saving the "world" on his own, or with the aid of organization alone, without God, would have been, and is, absurdity and arrogance. With God it is true service, commitment, and love, and opens itself to wonder, awe, and reflection on our insufficiency and God's greatness, the Creator's direction.

The sliver of moon has set, and the star/planet Venus lowers to the horizon. The owl hoots across the river. Everything is even more silent now and the silence can almost be heard. Another hoot, low and vibrant from across the river, farther away. A long pause of silence, like a breath of cool air after exertion, and a distant hoot, a double hoot far off south across the river in the dark woods. Then just dark woods, the tips of the trees across the river barely visible as dark marks on darker background.

This afternoon the canoe glides silently across the calm river water which is moving very slowly. Among the bulrushes near shore there is little movement. The ducks are almost all gone south as are most of the Canada geese. The ducks were not too visible in their flights, most having flown by night, but the geese have been honking their way over the past few weeks. It is most pleasant, and exciting, to hear the distant honks, and see the morning formation of geese, the honking louder, the wing beats regular, the whole constantly changing V moving toward the south.

On the river now things are not quiet. We paddle across and I cast a large wooden lure, reel it in and cast again, toward a group of fallen trees whose branches disappear in the deep water. No fish this time. I had seen a musky roll here a few days ago, and I will return here and fish again in anticipation of at least a "follow" by the musky, a look as it moves behind the lure.

But the river is too lovely, reflecting both banks of color in its still water today, for much other than just enjoying it.

We move slowly past the beaver house on the south bank and drift a while, hoping to see the beavers. This past spring there were several young, and they may be playing around the area in their preadolescence. The sky is clear with wispy high clouds, cirrus, in the shape of brush strokes. Mare's tails, they have been called, and usually presage a change in the weather within 24 hours or so. That is due to the high winds aloft, at probably 30,000 feet or more, which form them and shape their ice crystal mass. The water reflects these white ephemeral looking clouds with the brilliant colors of the trees along the banks.

We hear a honking of geese far south down the river. We watch but see nothing. The honking continues and finally, low on the water, a solitary Canada goose beats toward us, emitting a honk every few seconds. It passes, neck stretched, all alone, and disappears up river, the honking fading into the silence around us.

There are leaves on the river floating along with us, and occasionally, as I cast, the lure picks up a leaf on the retrieve. It may seem tedious, but the leaves are still colored brightly, and it's like plucking surprising colors out of a crayon box or paint selector chart. Every leaf is slightly different in shape and color. Every one will either sink or float down river to the dam, and then wash ashore or eventually freeze into the ice of the river. Perhaps there is a minute chance of a leaf reaching the Great Lakes, or eventually the Mississippi and finally the Gulf of Mexico. Unlikely, but possible.

Once, when we were cooling our feet in a pretty, quick, cool rocky bottom stream on a hot Saturday afternoon, my young daughter lost a sandal in the fast moving water. I chased it a few feet but couldn't catch it. She was fascinated by the idea that the sandal could conceivably reach the Gulf of Mexico. "And be eaten by a shark," she said; the loss of the sandal was not so bad after that.

A few strokes of the paddle now bring us to the cove, and we glide to shore. Here in the shallower water you can see the leaves on the bottom. Most won't get to the ocean, but it is nice to see them ghostly colored on the sand in the clear water.

The sun rose this morning in a thrust of splashed yellows, ochers, golds, and ambers, touching clouds which formed curling scenes on the sky. It was intense on the horizon, and the perception of it was so warm, although the air was cool, that for a moment you could not feel the cold.

The clouds, dark blue on the western side, moved quickly in from the west and shut the sun out. Then it rained. First, though, some sprinkling, but then it rained. Steady and angled in straight looking lines, knocking leaves from trees and puddling the road. Along the gravel edges tiny rivers ran with the brownish red dust turning them into paint.

The rain fell for about half an hour, hissing along the trees and tattooing the roof. Then it began to subside, and small breaks formed in the clouds, with bright blue patches visible.

The clouds began to break up, and as they did, a rainbow formed against the blue/gray western clouds, while the sun turned clear the sky. It was a very clear rainbow, especially well delineated. It made me look in awe. The rainbow lived a long time, about 15 minutes. It began to fade as the rain clouds dissipated and the sun rose higher, its delicacy devoured by the bright sunlight that originally gave it birth. A glorious start to a new day.

Biblically, the rainbow is a sign from God, a sign of covenant and promise after the flood. It still is a sign and promise. It is, scientifically, a matter of prismatic refraction of sunlight through rain drops. The laws of nature being fulfilled. Effect of effect of effect of a cause, of God's laws, God's creation.

The rainbow is a sign, a promise, a fulfillment, though only a small one. But always there. Whenever there is light and airborne water there is a rainbow, but it depends on where we stand to be able to see it. Like how we accept and open ourselves to God's existence and His relationship with us. An omnipotent God, all loving, cannot ignore us by His very nature. It does depend, though, on where we want to stand to accept Him.

The rainbow is a sign. Truly a beautiful one. Like the sunrise, it is an obviously common phenomenon, but every time it occurs it is uncommon.

The sunrise occurs and occurs, for how many millions of years we don't know. Mankind has seen many sunrises, but they are never quotidian, never simply repetitious, never copies and common. They are always extraordinary, even the ordinary ones. It also depends on where you stand, and how you see.

While I was walking from the mailbox this afternoon, the sky darkened to a stormy blue in the west, and a few drops of rain began to fall. They were cold, those drops that struck my face and hands, and they presaged colder weather. Soon the raindrops stopped, leaving, only for an instant, wet spots on the crushed gravel road. But a few minutes afterward the air was filled with sleet, little balls of icy snow pelting down, until the air was hazy white and my hat, jacket, and pants were coated with white spots until they melted away. The woods disappeared for a few minutes behind the white curtain of sleet, and then it stopped suddenly, and the woods came back, uncovered, as it were, by a vertical blanket.

The sky still looked threatening dark, blue cloudy, but the burst of wind was gone and nothing fell. I walked on to the curve of the road before the house. On the edge of the lawn one grouse pecked at some food. She looked around occasionally, but kept busily pecking at whatever food that was so desirable.

She walked about alone, somewhat unusual, because the grouse are covey animals, and simply looked quite comfortable strolling about on the lawn. Perhaps there were other grouse in the brush and woods nearer, but when I made too sudden a move in attempting to get close, she burst away in the typical bombastic fashion of grouse, and there were no others flying away. She climbed quickly, turning into what looked like an impenetrable mass of brush and young trees, penetrated it, and was gone.

Later the deer came, this time two does and two fawns, the latter the twins we've often seen. They fed some more on the acorns beneath our large oak. Before dark they were joined by the shy four-pointer, who nervously jumped every time an acorn fell near him or hit him. They pawed gently at the acorns on the ground, flicked their tails occasionally and looked around alertly, but in a relaxed manner. Chewing the acorns, they looked like domesticated creatures contentedly chewing cud in a pasture. The deer fed for over an hour in the yard, then moved gradually into the woods. Like the evening light, they just faded into the woods.

Yesterday afternoon the blue jays came calling, literally, yelling and calling out as they landed in the yard to eat some scraps we had thrown out. Their blue, black, and gray white color combination, and their raucous, aggressive manner, makes them very noticeable and interesting.

Soon they were joined by several very cautious crows, and much later, when there seemed to be no movement in the area, a large raven, with a four-foot wing span at least, hovered in under the oak tree. It stood silently looking about, its black feathers gleaming, and then, in a most comical manner, it hopped sideways toward a bit of remaining scrap food. It looked carefully around again, its sloping forehead ending in the big slightly curved, dark beak pointing toward the woods, like the stereotype bookkeeper with tiny spectacles, peeking through them.

The raven hopped like this several times, each time sideways, and each time both feet together, always carefully and suspiciously searching the area. Finally it reached its goal and picked something up in its beak and flew gracefully, with smooth, long, black, shiny wing beats, rowing away over the road into the woods. I think it was smiling.

The skies are gray and dark more often, and for longer periods these days as the sun sets sooner and rises later and the showers fall. Sometimes the winds bring short cold rain, and as we approach winter, sleet and snow flurries occur. The leaves of the deciduous trees keep falling, although some of the trees are completely bare already.

The weeds in the woods and the field are brown and shrunken, and the lawn no longer needs mowing. Two very plump grayish fox squirrels chased each other over the lawn today, one "chucking" every time it landed during its run. These were the fattest wild squirrels I've ever seen. The city squirrels, those living in trees in residential areas, usually are also quite sleek.

They chased around for a while, then suddenly ran up separate trees and quieted. The woods and their animals are quieting for the winter. Quieting in one sense, but maintaining almost frantic feeding most of the time.

We've had more bear droppings on the lawn, and the bear that has been visiting us tore down a beehive near the house, just into the woods near our yard. All we found were the bits and pieces of the gray hive and parts of the honey comb. The hive had been hanging about seven feet high on a rather thin branch and, of course, the bees had abandoned it some time ago. The bear may not have gotten any honey. I was hoping to.

We are also hoping to get a look at the bear in the daytime, so we have placed a few scraps of food in the yard. Perhaps the bear will visit in the day. They are preparing for their long hibernation, like some other animals in the woods, such as the squirrels and skunks, and to some extent the raccoons, woodchucks, and some smaller rodents. Many animals will be quite active, though.

The bears have had an excellent crop of blackberries and blueberries, some of it along our gravel road, much of which we have eaten. They are omnivorous and will probably have little trouble filling up and fattening for their winter's sleep.

The clouds moved in from the west as the sun set, and although at ground level it is calm, they are moving rapidly. The moon has risen, and it is very mild for mid-October. From the deck I can see the glimmer of moon on the river and the clouds rolling in. The pines on both sides of the house and the slope of the hill to the river stand identically tall, unmoving, not even a whisper of needles. It is so quiet I can hear the rattling fall of an acorn through the drying leaves of the old oak in the front yard.

Faintly, very faintly, I hear a high-pitched sound, long and drawn out, and try to listen more carefully. Again it barely touches me. Then silence. Standing on the deck later I listen again and hear it more clearly, bugle clear but distant—a coyote's howl. Soon I hear an answering howl, somewhat closer. Even the moon and wind pause as this duet plays on for about an hour, off and on, pause and repeat. It is mellow and lovely and wild. Once on a fog-bound lake early in the morning, we listened to coyotes call from one side of the lake to the other. There were several in each chorus, and the sound moved through the fog and over the lake like a knife, like a visible entity besides an aural one. It was lovely and wild, and yet a song of connectedness. It was a stern serenade in a most perfect orchestral hall. They were probably hunting, and the result would be the death of another animal—prey and predator. But something about that reflects the original Fall, the movement from special grace to search for grace, for everything has been affected.

Wolves howl, and theirs is a mellifluous timbre, a deep, long song. The coyotes are high pierced, a soprano to the wolves' bass or lead. These songs are part of the wilderness, but even more so a part of an understanding of where we live.

I thank "brother coyote," as St. Francis may have said, and go into the house, the moon fading behind the clouds and swiftly reappearing, the wind rising and humming through the tree tops, where moments before it was calm.

The woods are fairly "open" now, with most of the leaves gone, but there remain dry, hard, rusty colored oaks and maples, and a few birch and aspen in their saffron leaves. The elms and oaks are quite bare, and much of the low brush also. The curtain has pretty much disappeared from the woods, and you can see quite deeply. The ground squirrel rustling about in the leaves is visible at some distance, where in the summer it would have to be within a few feet to be visible.

The deer are difficult to see as they wear their grayish brown winter camouflage. Two bucks, the spike and the fourpointer, two does, and three fawns were in the yard under the oak, eating acorns this afternoon. They are sleek and healthy looking. Two red pine squirrels, which live in the large oak, rush about from deer to deer to eat the crumbs of acorns that fall from their mouths. They hurry about, their reddish tails swaying, picking a crumb here and there, turning sometimes in midrush to run to another deer. Later the grouse come, and the chickadees and juncos and blue jays will work the area for remaining crumbs, as will the ground squirrels, chipmunks, and mice. Perhaps what is left will be food for some insects, and from that, the leftovers will be eaten by microscopic, amoebic creatures.

Like the body of a dead woodchuck, which slowly, or rather quickly but imperceptibly, broke down, until only the bones remained, and they too finally disappeared into the earth and atmosphere, every bit of "stuff" breaks down. Life doesn't. Just the concrete "stuff" of it. Richard Eberhart's poem, "Groundhog," touches the question thoughtfully and awesomely.

The ruffed grouse are back under the oak, and the male is strutting about, tail feathers spread turkeylike, with muted colors, but still rich, and the ruff on the back of his head pointed out, as are his neck and throat feathers. He doesn't forget to look for acorn bits, though. The deer return. Two bucks, two does, and now all four fawns. The grouse do not move away, but strut their dance, at least the male does, but he attracts no attention this time.

The larger buck, the four-pointer, suddenly decides he doesn't want the others there, and lowers his antlers and brushes the fawns lightly, chasing them away, then the does trot into the woods with the fawns. The spike buck goes on eating, while the four-pointer stands alone in the middle of the yard. Soon he and the spike buck follow the trail the others took into the woods.

The gray squirrels, often fox squirrels with gray and red phases, which live nearby, appear also. They are very playful, running about and chasing each other, their large fluffy tails waving behind them as they shoot through the fallen leaves finding acorns. The pine squirrels, in the oak trees, chatter rapidly at them, and occasionally run down to claim an acorn or two, and hurriedly return to the oak. The grays ignore them; of course, the little pine squirrels are very quick. They spend much time chattering at the grays and waving their tails threateningly.

The grays finally leave, jumping along the woods, scattering dry leaves and making as much noise as a larger animal. As they leap and jump away, a cottontail bursts from the mint plants alongside the house, and runs toward the woods, but stops suddenly in the middle of the yard and begins to nibble. He then hops casually into the woods disappearing, except for his white tail, which remains visible for some time until it simply fades away. When the pine squirrels are satisfied they still claim the area, they go back to their own playful scampering around the acorns.

As the light dims, a very calm evening begins, and Venus appears as suddenly as someone switching it on, although it's probably just that I didn't notice. The river surface is picture still, calm and quiet, not even a swirling fish or insect mark on it. The silence is awesome, and pleasant, almost an active thing. From far down the river there is a sound, a jumbled call or cry. As it gains in intensity, it becomes clearer and turns into the aggressive honking of Canada geese. They are flying along the river, just several feet above the surface, and besides their raucous honking, the sound of their wings rowing the air is evident, almost a loud rustling. There are at least a hundred, and the sound of honking becomes encompassing as it echoes through the woods. They continue upriver at our cove, and the rustling of wings, punctuated by the continuous honking, gradually fades into just an echo. I can hear them faintly far away up river now, and it is, again, a sound of the north woods, and one that brings a pleasant sense of memory of adventures and tranquility juxtaposed.

Early this afternoon, with a hazy sky and clouds slowly moving in from the west, I stepped out the front door, facing the yard with its large oak and the driveway. On the left to the west northwest is a hill, about 30 feet high with a sandy bank facing us. I have used it as a backstop for very occasional rifle shooting, and for casual bow shooting. Several bales of hay and a target stand in front of the sand bank.

As I stepped out from the door, not yet in sight of the sandy slope, I heard a yelp, and stopped to look out under the oak. Nothing there but a grouse feeding quietly. So I stepped further, and walked toward the slope, and a movement caught my eye. On the slope, no more than 30 or 40 feet away sat a red fox, watching me carefully, his long tail hanging down the slope. I froze and watched him. With the rusty brown of the dried ferns and the sandy background, the fox was well camouflaged. The only reason I saw him was because he turned his head. His coat was light reddish, his tail a deeper red, and just before the white tip, the red darkened to almost pure black. The white tip, with this contrasting color next to it, looked very bright. This fox is different from the other two we've seen.

After we watched each other a few minutes, the fox stood up and slowly walked up the hill, keeping a wary eye on me, then walked into the dried brush among the tall white pines on the hill top. Seeing the fox that close was an exciting experience, and certainly another lesson in camouflage.

Shortly after the fox had moved into the woods, the sound of a burst of wing beats came from the top of the hill, and a grouse whizzed about three feet over my head toward the oak tree in the yard. The fox may have flushed her, and perhaps the fox had seen the grouse originally under the oak, and was "planning" an approach to it when I appeared and spoiled its plans. Nature's continual hunt goes on, even in people's yards, and if the grouse were taken by the fox in my front yard, it would have been no different than if it had been taken deep in the woods. It would have been eaten almost totally. Hunting for pleasure, although I have hunted quite a bit, is a sport, and the hunt is exciting, but its place on the scale of priorities is rather low, far below the simple enjoyment of the natural world around us.

There are other uses for the "woods" too, and one can take advantage of the economic element. One's woods could be used to great advantage in just enjoying them as they are, rather than always taking economic advantage of them as some of society expects. Of course, to use them economically is valid, as their resource is necessary. How we do it is important also.

I am looking for fox tracks in the sand more often these days since the recent sighting of the fox on the sand hill, and have, on a few occasions, spotted their tracks near the house. With some luck and patience, not necessarily in that order, I may be able to get a picture of the fox.

I have also been looking for bear tracks in the sand, but have not seen any yet. The bears will be hibernating in another month or so, and I'm hoping to see one in the yard. I don't want to bait them. So I'll just have to wait and hope to see one in the day. There have been more bear droppings in the yard, so a bear, perhaps not the same one, is feasting on acorns and other foods in the area.

This afternoon the wind increases from the northwest and pushes lines of low clouds that mass into an almost solid overcast of gray blue ceiling. It is strictly autumn cloud, pregnant with snow or sleet, and charging along undeviatingly from the northwest. When the sun breaks through occasionally it shines on baring trees and brightens white birch stems with only a few red leaves of maples, yellows of ashes, and elms, hickory, and ironwood, and the deep gold dried rust of large leaved red oaks, like the one in our yard, which retains its leaves long into the winter.

The sounds of the woods now include the crinkling of dry leaves together, in that percussion section of woods' orchestras, and the sound of cold branches snapping in concert. The ground is almost completely covered with dried leaves, and when the clouds let go their burden, the sleet stings down onto your face and you can hear each bit of sleet strike the leaves. The leaves quiver when struck by the sleet, and the sound becomes almost a hissing. Flurries like this stop very quickly. Later they will consist not of sleet but snow, which is silent but more efficient at hiding everything. The flurries stop and start as silently as the moon sets or the seasons change, although they too are accompanied by certain sounds familiar and particular to the specific season. When the sleet falls, it lasts for only a few moments on the warmer ground or leaves, and soon melts away leaving tiny darker wet spots, which soon dry. The snowflakes that fall in these flurries, hesitatingly, as though they are testing the area, also melt and leave spots of moisture. But soon the snow won't be falling in these tentative ways, soon it will be directly and unmitigatingly firm. And it will cover the ground and the leaves and the brush and the branches of the trees; it will cover ant hills, and tiny burrows, and burrows with mounds of earth at the lip, and small caves, uprooted trees, crevices, cracks, and drives and houses. It will be purposeful snow.

Down by the cove the wind just tips the water into activity. Above the river a red-tailed hawk soars in perfectly executed downwind and upwind turns, maintaining position and singing out in a long screaming call every once in a while. Two crows fly by, one on each side of the river, black against the gray blue dark of clouds, calling to each other and to anyone who hears. The cove reflects them for a moment. Then the hawk curves into view on the mirror of water, and the wind ruffles it away.

The water of the cove is exceptionally clear today. The bottom is covered with fallen leaves, and the shore is lined deeply with fallen pine needles. A few small bits of cedar and spruce lie on the shoreline at the bottom. The bulrushes are brown and withered looking, and bend almost to the water in driving gusts of wind.

The shores of the cove are an encyclopedic collection of floating materials that reflect the seasons quite clearly. Now in the fall the debris consists of leaves and pine needles washed across the river during a southwesterly wind.

In the summer it is water weeds, dead mayflies, in season by the thousands, a great variety of twigs, cottonwood seeds and other seeds in fluffy white carriers. When the weeds cluster on the shore and surface of the water after a long period of southerly winds, the frogs play on the shore and in the water, and bounce over the short grass. Most are leopard frogs, and are green spotted, and alive in curved energy and graceful leaps, with long powerful legs. They make colored green arcs in the air.

Now the weeds are gone, and the pine needles pack the cove's shoreline, and the bottom is carpeted with the leaves of all the trees in the woods that have been deracinated to the ground and the water.

When the wind changes to the north or northwest as it has now, the pine needles will move out into the current very slowly and disappear, and the cove will be clear again on the shore. Soon after, the water will move many of the leaves on the bottom slowly toward open water and the current. And then the cove will slowly freeze into winter.

Across the river the bare trees bend, and the pines, and firs, and spruce whistle in the wind, and bow. The birches are bright exclamation marks on the black river, and the wind pushes the gray blue clouds over quickly into the calming dark of night.

A fox den. No more than 100 yards from the house down the east trail. I discovered it while taking a walk, when I found some more fresh bear droppings. I stooped and looked around the area for more sign, and there, about 15 yards from me, was the den, a dark hole in the side of a hill with brush piled above it. The entrance would be, and was, invisible in the summer, and it was pure luck that allowed me to see it now. It looks like a fox den, and appears to be the right size. We have had foxes in the area, and their tracks have been visible in the sandy sides of our drive. When the snow stays we will be able to tell. The earth in front of it has been padded down quite well, so it has been in use for some time. We are looking forward to observing the den area, without getting too close, and perhaps next spring some young foxes will be there.

Last night the northern lights flashed and glowed across the sky, even directly overhead. The aurora borealis are caused, as far as we know, by the ionization of electrons in the atmosphere by charged particles, or energy from sun storms. The sun storms and other natural electrical activity cause difficulty with radios and other electrical functions, but when the northern lights appear, caused by these same particles, they are often magnificent. Last night they were sheets of pale green and white, and they would fade slightly only to burst again in streaks of sheets of crisp light on the sky. Sometimes the light is so bright you can read by it. The northern horizon was bright with a steady glow, and the streaks of light continued for several hours. It is silent, yet symphonic.

Over the tamarack swamp to our east, the yellowed needles of these trees even glowed orange gold in the light from the sky.

In the day the tamarack needles, which turn a lovely yellow in fall, and most fall off (the only conifer that sheds its "leaves" in the autumn), glow in the sun. The light from the aurora made them glow again, in a different gold, a ghostly glow of dull orange and yellow, as if lit from inside, a neon flow, but cold, like coming winter.

The northern lights faded late, and the sky was again occupied with myriad pin-point stars, so great in number, so prodigiously spread upon the black of sky, that it always brings a sense of awe. Simply the contrast between the black sky and the sharp lights of diamond white stars is magnificent. There is not a thought between them, among these great masses, and apparently comparatively tiny things that sparkle and glow. But there is in our small, also comparatively insignificantly sized mind. Not just brains, the physical component of the mind, but "mind" itself, the intellectual consciousness and conceptualization and free will elements of the self. The Director of all this symphony of sight, sound, and sense deserves a bow, and much, much, more.

I caught a loud "yuk-yuk" sound off to my side in the woods and stopped, staring hard to see its source. A large dark bird leaped from the side of a tree near me, and flew heavily over my head to stop on the side of a tree not 20 feet away. It was the pileated woodpecker, big as a crow, even bigger, black and white and gray, designed almost like a harlequin, with a red bright crest and long gold bill. The pileated woodpecker is dressed in formal wear, and its size and distinct shape and color are wonderful to see in the woods.

We have other woodpeckers, all beautiful and interesting in their own way. The downy and hairy woodpeckers, very similar in color, the hairy somewhat larger than its cousin the downy, and the red-headed woodpecker, are very common here in the Midwestern north woods. But the pileated still is exciting to see—large and colorful. It livens the woods more than most other single birds, mostly because it is so visible, and its strikingly shaped head and neck, with the flame bright red crowned crest, is awesomely visible.

Another north woods fall morning—Saturday. The fog so fills the air that visibility is limited to 20 or 30 feet outside the house. After a while it lifts slowly and hangs in the trees, a very low cloud ceiling looking as though it had been painted a pearl gray/white. It is almost iridescent. To raise one's head from contemplative prayer on this quiet morning, and turn to the window, and see on the rail of the deck a grouse looking through the window, or perhaps looking at its reflection, is a surprise. I can study it quite leisurely: the distinct and geometrically arranged bars along the wings, the tail feathers, clumped together now, but still displaying the bars, or hint of bars, of various shades. Its ruffed head is perfectly formed and quickly turns in sharp, well-defined moves. Finally, the grouse fidgets, ruffling its neck feathers, and spreading its wings partially, leaps off the deck rail, the rapid loud rustling, almost a roaring takeoff, similar to the flush of the bird in the brush.

It is gone into the pearly air by the pines. How can it maneuver in such fog at the speed of its flight? The fog hangs, glowing pearl, nascent touch of higher altitude sky, a private secret realm in which one revels, hidden.

Later, early in the afternoon, back by the living room windows, not just a fox. It is the golden one, the palominocolored fox I've seen before. Lying in the weeds, which now are bent down, on the slope to the river, 30 feet from the house. If the weeds were high, it may not have been visible.

As it is, the fox rises to a sitting position, and with its left hind leg scratches its neck, furiously, the leg a blur. It scratches on and on, turning its head and neck slightly. Then suddenly it stops, stretches out the magnificent tawny tail with the white spot on the end, and begins to lick and clean its front paws, bending its muzzle, turning the smooth black legs, cleaning the rich black fur. It does this for almost five minutes without pause.

This is the fox's late Saturday morning casual awakening, its bath and clean up, its preparatory ritual and primp before Saturday's hunt. It finally rises, trots rapidly around, sniffing the ground, sniffing the air, black ears, black as the four legs, pointed straight and alert. Then turning a circle, it lies down in the weeds again, to lick and brush the gold along its sides. It snaps at a fly or other insect in the air, stands slowly to stretch, a gold, black, and white arc in the weeds.

The fox then trots off into the woods, bright and quick, disappears into the darkness of trees, white spot on the rich tail the last thing I see of it. This was not just a mousing machine—it is far more—yet less than the source of thought and concept and free will reflection in the mind that enjoyed seeing and possessing, for a short time, that golden fox.

The air is filled with a rhythmic "yuk, yuk, yuk" as I step out the front door. As I search for the sound, a now familiar voice of the pileated woodpecker, another "yuking" joins in from the woods on the left, and across the drive fly two pileateds, their red crests wild on their black and white bodies. The eye is attracted so startlingly to these red areas. They fly with their strong wing beats to the trees on the right of the drive. Both choose separate trees and commence rapid pecking. They stand on the sides of the trees, almost vertically, strong feet and talon-like toes into the trees. Heads with red crests become momentary blurry streaks as they hammer through the bark.

They leave together, black wings and a spot of red through the trees, their "yuk" call echoing. Then the woods are silent. Soon, though, I'm sure, there will be other movement.

Early November rain is purposeful and sharp, slashing down, mixed with occasional soft large wet snowflakes. The rain slants, and the gusts of wind are icy. The early fall rains are gentle and warmish, but these later rains precede and signal the snowfalls and arctic winds with heavy gusts that cut and freeze. The rain now has a minute taste of that, just a hint of winter's smell, and the sharp, tiny feel of cold air and fast driving snowfall. The cold rain pounds on the roofs and clanks against the windows. It is a good evening to be in bed early, warm under the quilts, with the chill rain lashing the house and the woods, with its prescience of snow and winter, under a pewter sky almost touching the tallest wind-whipped trees.

The large soft snowflakes dive out of an off-white sky, which dims the horizon and fades the tops of pines. There is very little wind now, and it is one of those times you open your mouth and catch big snowflakes on your tongue no matter how old you are.

As the wind abates by the river, the snowflakes touch silently on the water and are gone. They stay on the colder ground, and sit on the tops of fluffy dried weeds and pine needles and branches. I walk toward the house, enjoying the white on white of snowflakes against the sky, and I taste the snowflakes. A vague shape appears above me, and out of the cloud of snow up high, a Canada goose glides, wings perfectly still, like a ghost, and turns gracefully through the falling snow, neck straight, cups its wings slightly and lands along the brown bulrushes on the river. Everything has been so silent, the whole act, as though it had been rehearsed. The goose dark in the white cloud, white snow, silent sky; things happening in total silence. Whispers of things. The significance was one of beauty captured, a painting, a poem. There was also something more of order and cause and effect. The alignment of occurrences belies casualness. It probably happens all the time, but this time I was there to see. Also, I was there as part of the poem. And I was there to enjoy, feel awe, and ask why. I was there to see and feel something beyond just a goose landing out of a snowy sky. I was there to reason and ask why.

The goose is hidden in the bulrushes, and I walk back toward the house, with large white snowflakes appearing out of the broad white sky. Thomas Aquinas said, "nature leads to grace." If we allow our inherent rational direction to move freely in the direction of grace, it does. If we remain unprejudiced and open to the transcendental, to the Creator, it will. Nature leads to the sublime "why," which leads to the Sublime, God.

This is not a pantheistic sense of appreciation, or adoration, of nature. It is awareness of, and a movement to, creation, to sources, to ultimate sources and beginnings. The goose gliding soundlessly through the snowy sky to land in the river is a moment, a fraction in time, a certain order and harmony which strikes us, those particularly who are unprejudiced as to sources, and we, through an inherent quality sourced from something higher than us, react to its awareness in us. The poetry is found in our souls, and doesn't develop itself. The dignity we feel is beyond us, and comes to us, and we must open ourselves to the source, the Creator.

I will go again and read Gerard Manley Hopkins's poem, "God's Grandeur." Hopkins has excellent vision.

This morning every twig, every branch, every evergreen needle, every weed stalk is covered with snow. It is falling very gently but firmly, and the snow looks like it will stay the winter.

A first heavy snow is always awesome. Part of it is the brightness of white on dark greens and browns and rusts in the woods. The pine boughs are heavy with snow and droop gently, while the weeds close to the ground are being pressed to lie closer before frigid winds force them to hide near the ground. The juncos with their slate gray/black upper bodies and white breasts and bellies hop around joyfully, feeding in the shallow snow. They, like the chickadees and nuthatches, are the most cheerful of winter companions outdoors. Every morning they are here exploring, chirping, and greeting the day.

Every morning also now the cove has a very thin sheet of ice on it, developed in the colder night, and during the day it usually melts, but lately the ice has become surreptitiously thicker, and lasts throughout the day. It is as though the winter is gaining small footholds, or toeholds, whenever possible. The ice, one cold manifestation of frigidity. The gentle current of the river, limited to its center for all practical purposes, does not affect the forming of ice, especially on the cove, with its calm and quiet water protected by the bulrushes and trees.

As you walk to the cove from the house, the birches across the river, pale white columns resting at angles slightly other than the vertical, reflect off the black morning water clearly, mirror perfect, but when the ice comes, it casts their reflection in a mottled haze, a ridged frostiness that is a signature of the cold.

The other night, visiting the cove, with only the stars lighting it, I saw a muskrat swim quietly across, back and forth, until it finally noticed me, a few feet away, and vanished, leaving a gentle confusion on the glass of black water. The stars undulated in the reflection until the tiny ripples calmed, moving silently under the edge of early ice along the shore.

Soon the ice will thicken and spread out to the center of the river when the cold comes forcefully. But it will be thinner there, where the current still moves gently.

Now, though, the ice is strengthening its hold, its sign, on the water. And the afternoon clouds come in low, and swift, and heavy, the wind escalating to occasional hammer blows, and the pine boughs, which bend over and down and swing back when the hammer of wind withdraws, are being exercised heavily. This cold wind and cloudy pewter sky presage the hard snow of real winter, rather than the tentative snowflakes and short cold snaps of fall.

In the woods an occasional crash signals the break of rotten branch or tree top and its fall to the ground, scattering and clattering through the branches. While the snow begins to pile on the ground and "whites" out the forest floor, it is still possible, this late in the season, to find, tucked under a fir or spruce, a bright green small fern, like the fiddleback. With the north side protected from the winds, and the south exposed to the sun, even partly, a tiny fern stays bright spring green with snow building around it. It is an amazing sight—so out of place, seemingly, but so delightful to see and later to be aware of. It is like a bright song at a time when a song lifts spirits.

This enchanting fern, hiding in a tiny cranny in the great woods, flourishing when most others are dormant, sings of light and brightness. The snow will soon cover it, but what a glory. What a gift to see! What a greater gift to share that joy of seeing with someone else. We can perceive the hand of the Creator again and contemplate in awe.

"Let All the Earth Cry out With Joy to the Lord," sings Psalm 66 in the Old Testament. Indeed, it does, and we should too.

The streaks of ice blue green lightened the northern sky first, in sheets of movement you could almost hear. Then white and pale blue lights brightened the whole sky, even the southern horizon. Soon the entire expanse of visible sky was filled with gyrating, undulating ripples of glowing lines and streaks of aurora borealis, the northern lights. The center of the sky glowed red in varying intensities and brightnesses, and I had never seen as bright and colorful and widespread a display as this evening's. The moon, rising in the east, was overwhelmed by this electronic lighting of the atmosphere. It was a weakly pale orb, in contrast to the neon bright ionic bursts of color and flashes of brilliance on the sky. But they, the moon and the aurora, still looked lovely together!

The wind hissed gently through the pines, and other than that occasional sound, nothing could be heard, and the glow from the sky was silently magnificent, and we watched for at least an hour. My face, upturned, felt delicate touches of crystal ice fall. The sky was only slightly hazy in the west but the crystalline clouds participated, it seems, in the great display. Beauty has more than a name, and where does it come from?

This morning a light snow covered the ground, about an inch, and the river showed a break in a line through its center, the rest having frozen enough to hold the snow. When the sun rises, it will probably melt much of the new ice, but the ice has its winter grip on the river close to shore. On the road to the mailbox a bear stopped, and the heat from its body melted a right rear footprint into the fresh snow. I followed the tracks a bit into the woods and then headed back to the road, excited that I had found the tracks. The bear was probably no more than 180-200 pounds, and was probably ready for hibernation. At least it will be within a few weeks that the bears will seriously seek their winter dens. I still have not seen one this year and am hoping to before the heaviest winter. Of course, the chances of seeing one next spring ought to be quite good.

The bears seem to have had good eating this year. Certainly, to the bear's omnivorous appetite, almost any year provides grand fulfillment. But this fall the berries were exceptional, both in quality and quantity, and other vegetation and small mammals were plentiful.

This afternoon I stood on the hill, alongside the house, in a couple of inches of fresh snow. The sky was winter sharp blue, almost an opalescent azure, and it reflected on the strip of open water in the river below. The ice has advanced from either side of the river until only that thin strip of water remains visible. The contrast between the black, blue water, and the fresh snow covered ice, is striking. For some reason I stopped walking and quietly stood to hear the silence. Not a sound can be heard. It is like being washed by a cooling shower of rain on a hot day. The pines and spruce alongside me do not move, not a needle. The silence is like a huge valley. It is almost permeable. It can be felt; it is loneliness and calm and wilderness and sybaritic all at the same time. It is a silence of something. Not a vacuum. It has some kind of essence. A silence of being not just void. It has substance but an ethereal one. The contemplative, open to the highest good, can not only see that but becomes intimately aware of it.

Does not God speak in whispers?

Soon I began to feel the cold seep into the soles of my feet. A very gentle wind stirred the tops of the pines to make a tenuous sigh. The silence has not been oppressive, rather it has been enlightening and freeing. I have heard it. The contemplative seeks silence to eliminate obstacles to God's presence—I'm beginning to see why.

Looking out the window over the river while eating breakfast, I saw movement in the sky beyond the river. A tiny speck, which soon resolved itself into a bald eagle soaring over the trees, and a few times dipping below the horizon of pine tree tops, gusting up across the river. The eagle made several very sharp and steep banks, exposing its tremendous winged silhouette and its white head and tail, then circled wide and moved up river out of sight.

This appears to be a bit late for eagles to remain in the area, since most migrate at least a bit farther south, where some open water is, or may be, available. Of course, this eagle may be hunting near a dam below which there is usually open water all year. I am looking forward to seeing it again, and it may be one of a pair my daughter saw this summer near a perch and large nest, not far from the house, on the river.

WINTER

THIS AFTERNOON WAS delightful, with a gentle southerly breeze and some high cirrus clouds out of an azure sky. The temperature was about 35 to 40 degrees and the grouse were taking advantage of it in the yard. One grouse very often visits the small flowering crab tree in the middle of the yard. Today, I saw it in the tree's small branches. It was balancing like a tight rope walker, occasionally stretching and picking at a bud on a branch. This balancing act resulted in many furious and frantic flurries of wings to maintain position on the thin branches. The grouse performed this way, moving about the tree, for 30 minutes or so. A pleasant show that ended when it finally leaped toward the ground and flew into the heavy cover east of the house, into its refuge of balsam and spruce and thicket. The fox that hunts this area has not been around, or rather I haven't seen him (or her), but it would be interesting to see its reaction to the dance of the grouse in the tree.

Last night, after a relatively warm day of about 40 degrees, the cold moved in, and by 10 pm, the temperature had dropped to 15 degrees F. The river, which had opened quite a bit in that warm air and sun, began to freeze rapidly in the sudden cold. There was no wind, so the cold settled in the lowest places, particularly the river.

When ice forms rapidly, or reforms as in this case, the ice grinds and rubs against itself and shifts and growls in its crystalline expansion. From this come enormous groans and creaks and sharp whip sounds which, to the uninitiated, are not natural and are often taken for otherworldly. It is a curious timpanic symphony, reflecting some of the north woods mystery.

This was an occasion of tremendous sounds from the ice of the river. Sharp snapping ricochet sounds like the cracking of a whip and its echo, and then the long receding ricochet sound, long drawn out yowls and screeches that sound like screams and groaning yelps and howls. There have been more than a few people who have locked their doors, and in one case that I know of, left the area, when hearing these sounds for the first time.

The sounds, during a calm cold night with almost utter quiet in the woods, raise the hairs on the neck at first, and do have an unearthly resonance. They continued last night long past dark into the early morning hours. As I lay in bed, I could hear them somewhat distantly through the window.

Often we would walk along the lakes at night, and pause for long moments, waiting for the voice of the frozen water, the sound of a very natural and normal event that provides us with a certain pleasure. Large lakes particularly are "noisy" this way, but it is a pleasant sound if you know what it derives from, and is another sign, and sense, of the north country.

Today the sky is milky and snowy looking. The air is calm and several inches of snow cover the ground. The blue jays fly back and forth, between the woods and the bacon grease bread we've thrown down below the deck. Occasionally, the snow buntings, juncos, and some sparrow-like birds, which appear to winter here, join in feeding with the blue jays. The jays, though, assert their dominance, and do not permit the smaller birds to stay too long. After a while the jays are overwhelmed by sheer numbers and fly back and forth raucously, probably storing some of the greased bread.

One jay has picked up a whole piece of bread, half soaked with grease, and flies toward the woods. Halfway there, and losing altitude because of his load, he turns down the hill toward the river, and furiously flapping, flies down to a tree below the slope from the house. After resting, this jay wings over in short hops from tree to tree, until it reaches the heavy woods.

The jays are noisy, flashy, and interesting to have around, with their various shades of blue and gray and their crested heads. They contrast well with the other winter birds like juncos and snow buntings that dash about in flocks and are quite friendly. The crows, of course, have personalities of their own and are fun to observe.

All the birds have their own offering, as do all the animals and the trees and flowers and weeds and fish and seeds. Their own gifts and their own offerings. And we can perceive God's work in creation, all the beauty evident of man and his relationship to nature around us, as well as the natural world itself. Were it not for man, who would do the analysis?

The evening is calm. Almost absolutely still with no wind, and the sounds carry long distances in the cold dense air. As twilight develops, the stillness becomes palpable and calming. The ice creaks now, and sometimes the whiplash snap of it echoes off among the trees, splitting the silence as thoroughly as a mallet splitting a frozen log.

In the woods, close to the house, a cottontail rabbit hops among the thorn thickets, barely visible in his brown and white camouflage. The snowshoe hare is quite invisible, unless you are able to see a bit of movement. The tracks of the larger snowshoe hare, obviously pointing to the source of its name, are further away from the house than the cottontail's, which stays very close to the house walls. I haven't seen a snowshoe hare yet this winter, but as I take more walks in the woods, I'm sure I will, but only if they move.

The dark is setting evenly across the sky and the woods as the clouds dissipate the light of the setting sun. A few flakes of gentle snow begin to fall, fresh and sharp on my face. There is still no wind, and the snowflakes fall slowly, undriven and roaming in their voyage to the ground.

I listen for coyotes howling among the falling snow, or for an owl hooting, but tonight there is no sound, only the silent fall of snow. Does snow striking the ground make sound? Perhaps; perhaps also it is good it doesn't appear to. The evening has turned to night, and I can only feel the gentle flakes of snow on my face and hands. The woods are silent. The quiet is, at the same time, openness and covering. It is a pleasant anomaly.

This morning the dawn light revealed, slowly, a frozen world, the river solid and its ice covering bared in spots by the wind. Only several inches of snow cover the ground, and the sky is the color of the snow below. The trees today are coated with frost, particularly the bare branches of deciduous trees. The first rays of the dawning sun strike the tops of the birch trees across the river from the cove. The sun creates a bright gold line on the hoary, frosted branches. It is like an inverted curtain exposing the lighted stage, everything on top glows, below it is dusky, dim.

The sun's rays move down the trees, illuminating the birch trunks, and livening the snow and ice on the river. It is a frozen golden scene, not the soft and mellow gold of autumn, but hard and solid gold, almost brittle in color. The juxtaposition of suprawhite frost on the trees, and the cold gold light of the winter sun, makes jewelry, winter special dawn jewelry, while rose gold-edged rounded mammarian clouds fly above the cold.

Three blue jays coast from a tree at the edge of the woods into the gold sunlight, to feed on the scraps we've thrown in the yard. They are quiet, but efficient, in this frigid dense air. A raven appears from over the roof of the house, over my head as I watch through the window, and circles easily in the good flying density of cold air. The raven croaks softly and joins the jays. They are alert, but do not seem to fear him.

Everything else appears dormant, and the sun climbs slowly higher, the catalytic agent for movement and warmth and life, limited and enclosed by cold in one sense, but vibrant and rich in essence. The winter is but another time, another situation, sometimes another challenge. And it, like the other seasons, is another aspect of variety and order. Nature doesn't prescribe laws. It is not conceptual or rational. It follows laws, the laws from the Transcendent source. The laws of biological human function are of nature, but the laws of morality, while partly reflective of nature, are also beyond it. They encompass nature, and nature manifests them, for they can only come from transcending nature, which includes mankind in its barest sense. Yet the soul, the essence of man, is a superior part of that creation, closest to the Creator, an immutable element.

The question of innocent suffering has been discussed and debated since the beginning and is vividly remembered at the sound of a rabbit's shriek as an owl strikes it. The question is answerable only if God is in the picture. It is answerable only if we realize that the suffering of Christ, the Revealed Word, in His obedience to God the Father, was a conscious emptying of self for God and man. Together, never alone—a definition of love—to die for and before the other. The suffering of innocent animals is different from mankind's, but perhaps it too must be an example of creation's misery after the Fall, after the act of resistance to God, the turning in to oneself, and this pain and suffering lead to the revitalized and reconstituted self in God at the end of history, the beginning of perfection in the transcendent sense. Someday it will be whole. God does not waste creation, and only a part of creation can waste itself. Only humans can be insouciant to God and to each other. Animals cannot. The God, who loves us so that He sent His Son to die for us, loves also His other creations.

One of our functions may be to wonder and to see. To contemplate means just that. That wonder, that contemplation rising, can also lead to love and commitment to God. It requires an act of humility, an act of fealty to God, to the awareness that there is the transcendent, and that humility leads to and from contemplation, awareness, seeing.

The beauty of nature then is more than just a mathematical effect. It is a connection, a connection to the rest of mankind, in sharing, awe, and God. The world, nature, does not explain itself; the beauty exists and needs an explanation. One does not adore nature; one adores the Creator, who makes Himself known through it in a superabundant manner. St. Thomas Aquinas explains this by the awareness that the whole good cannot be found in the realm of created things but in God alone. The reflection of the whole good, God, is found in those created things, and especially in us. Every living thing in some way reflects a glimmer of our life.

As I drive down the road, a simpler reflection is found in the predawn darkness where there is a bright light through the trees. At the curve and clearing it's very visible. The moon, glowing so brightly, so clearly I can distinctly see its large craters, gleams at me. The snow crystals reflect its blue white light. They liven the snow, and though you can see millions of them reflecting the moonlight during a short walk, every clear moonlit evening or night or morning, it is never boring, never uninspiring. This mounded snow is not soup. It is countless crystals. It is countless crystal mirrors. It is ineluctably, in its simple common way, always awesomely new.

The snow in its silence speaks visibly. The prints of tiny animals, the mice and moles, wander about in designs apparently planned. The larger animals and the birds leave their marks, and they are specifically identifiable to a point, and at the least they are indication of some creature's passing. The mysterious elements are always there: why did this rabbit stop here and suddenly hop in long stages into the brush pile. There are no other tracks around. Farther along the meadow in the woods is a sign of a possible reason. The wing tip marks of a hawk or owl, several depressions in the snow as though made by a fist, and finally a depression with a few drops of blood, the ephemeral record of the death of a mouse, food for the bird, completion of one cycle, continuance and semblance of order.

The snow melts, new snow piles on top of it. A clean ledger, an open page, the stuff of which mystery is made.

The pragmatic effect of snow is, of course, protection for the ground and plants below. The snow, architectural crystals, acts as insulation and is protective. An anomaly perhaps, but not to the unprejudiced. These common miracles are still miracles.

An early cold glides in during the night. Twenty below zero under clear, clean skies, where the stars are close enough to elicit surprise at their clarity, their icy brightness. The air is dense and sounds travel great distances. The river groaning and creaking in its ice coat, the snap and crash of a tree, its sap or water within it frozen to expansion, producing an explosion, cracking a large piece of it. There are other sounds to hear also: the owl's common hoot, the occasional scream of a rabbit caught by the owl or other predator, the distant yip of a fox, and in the day crows calling and a raven's croak, blue jays with their aggressive shrill-happy sounds, the friendly chickadees and juncos, the mad "yuk-yuk" of the pileated woodpecker, and many others. But in the night they are shrouded and mysterious.

Some of the sounds are inexplicable, at least to me. The cold seems to magnify some of them, too.

Even the sun's gold throughout the day cannot warm. It warms, but there is always the cold, in the shade, in a burst of breeze, or worse, a sharp wind. It is heavy and seemingly brittle. Yet despite the apparent unpleasantness, it is a season, and it can support happiness and joy, as all suffering supports joy. The cold presages the anticipatory awareness of spring, and prior to that the wonder and awe of Easter, the thanks of it.

The cold burns your face with the wind, makes you gasp when you breathe too heavily, is almost perceptibly concrete at times. But it fades also, is mutable and ephemeral. It also provides for excellent pleasant comparisons to the other seasons.

Sometimes it is surprising to see how wildlife survives the cold, but the animals do, if they are relatively well fed and somewhat protected. Some don't survive it. There is a reason.

The cold is sometimes a glimmer of nonessentialness, a negation reminding of the mutable: warm homes are special places, quotidian as they can be, but they are very special places when it is cold.

There is dark and white, but they both consist of many shades and colors. Some tall grasses sit against the snow in a dry gold. Branches of bushes contrast sharply in their black sticks with the shady light under the pines, and small weeds, shapes in clusters of roundheaded sticks, are gray/brown on the snow, in danger of being completely covered. And the snow, light and airy, weights enough on the spruce and balsam to bend their tips into graceful curves around their green on white to the sky.

The snow falls silently, heavily, and visibility is only a few hundred yards. This is no few inches of snow; it is going to be a foot at least. It covers and coats and rounds rough edges in the woods. It softens everything and bleaches and paints. There is white and green; the pines wear white frostings and ermine backs, the weeds delineate against the snow their own darkness, and the tree trunks are stark dark against white. This snow will coat the world soft, white, and silent.

Christmas at the cove is especially quiet, as though there were a solidity and concreteness to the love we must be aware of today. There is a distinct connection between the beauty here and the love, between the curve of river and the Birth. The balsam fir from outside goes inside, in decorative joy, with garlands, and candles, with light so we celebrate the Light. The scent of balsam, outside unnoticeable in the cold, swells the house with fragrance; it alone presages a connection between

God and man and the natural world we live in. There is also reason for the suffering here. There is reason for the suffering of the Child. The Fall of man affects all creation, all things. The Birth of Christ affects all things, too, in an even more ineluctably salubrious and total way. The chickadee does not know or understand the celebration of a 2000-year-old Birth. But when it dies, there will have been something, forever, for in God nothing is wasted. For man, image of creation and Creator, there will be more than just something. The Child born we celebrate today tells us—just by being born.

Without the Spirit, without the Light, there is only immeasurable emptiness, death. With it there is always life.

The Creator becomes incarnate, Jesus Christ, a human person, living in the world, in nature. It is an act of humility and love, and humility leads to contemplation, contemplation to reality, to more than transcendence, to the Creator. Christmas. God's investment in the finite can be trusted to infinity because it includes every created thing, and we can perceive that investment in some minute way, as He can fully. Christmas, the ineffable Word becoming visible, human, the superabundant act of love, like creation and the sacrifice on the cross. The act of Love, to die for and before the other!

Under the ice on the river, the water flows, and the snow falls on it very slowly, gently, and not a bit of air moves. Everything is suspended, even the water under the ice, which I cannot see. Only for a moment the house is visible through the gentle snowfall. But it is there; I walk toward it, making soft hissing sounds with my boots on the snow. Evening begins to occur.

This morning sun is bright, especially bright through the cold, very clear air. It is about 10 degrees above zero, and the snow crunches sharply under my boots on the road to the mailbox.

The deer have been active this morning, and their fresh tracks step across the road. Near the house are tracks of a weasel, hunting along the brush sticking out of the snow. It will be an ermine this time of year, pure white with a black tip on the tail. In the summer they are rich brown with white undersides. Very aggressive, weasels (ermine) will attack prey many times their size, and on one occasion in the summer an adult and three young weasels living near our house screeched hotly at me and made charging feints, to keep me away from their den in a hollow log lying on the ground. I've never seen one in the winter—that's obviously the purpose of their being all white. The black tail probably catches the eye of a pursuer and allows the ermine to escape more readily. At least only the tail becomes the prime offering for another predator.

About halfway down the road a deer stood up and walked rapidly deeper into the woods. She probably had been watching my approach as she lay about 20 feet from the edge of the road. My footsteps crunching along the snow gave her long warning.

Tiny ice crystals sparkle down from the frost-coated trees at every bit of slight wind. They reflect, as they fall and turn, the brilliant sun through this extremely clear, cold air. They fall silently, reflecting tiny bursts and flashes. Against the blue sky it is simply beautiful.

The cold air is sharp when I inhale heavily, and I walk along to the house, mail in hand, crunching gently on the snow, with waves and myriads of minute crystal explosions of light hovering all around me. The sky is infinite blue, and the shadows of trees in the woods are precisely clear blue-black.

Winter, deep winter, is in the north woods.

God is not elusive, it is we who elude his gift of Himself by our attention to everything else but Him. Silence and openness to Him—find Him! The contemplative act.

On the deck chickadees and nuthatches constitute most of the visitors to the bird feeder. They take turns. Only one bird at a time feeding. The others wait or signal their impatience with a dive toward the feeder.

The chickadees are so fearless they will come close to a person even in the deep woods, and they will soon feed from your hand, after gentle coaxing with a bit of bacon or seeds, if you are even only slightly patient. The chickadees flutter about, singing in their sharp little clicks, in the most cheerful manner, and with their contrasting gray, white, and black markings and handsome shape, they are most welcome around the area.

The cold has withdrawn and been replaced with surprisingly warm temperatures—a late January thaw. We walk along the edge of the frozen river, on a foot of softening snow, among pygmied bulrushes and cattail remains that stood thickly and verdantly in the summer. Now we walk on top of these bits of warm weather, crunching through the snow, exploring the little coves and bays, just feet across, that we couldn't reach in the summer by canoe.

In a few spots there are watery looking areas of snow, almost pale green. I step carefully there, even though this close to shore the water itself is only a foot or two deep. My foot crunches through a foot of ice and touches a few inches of water. The ice is rotten here because of springs pushing water up into these shallows of the river. The spring water is warm enough to keep the ice from freezing solidly, except in the most frigid weather.

Down along the shoreline the occasional wettish green spots reflect other springs, unknown and invisible in summer but bared pleasantly in the snow and ice which attempt, but don't succeed, in covering them.

The water from these springs is colder than the summer river and warmer than freezing. It is a constant in the revolution of seasons and times. Surreptitious springs fill the river along its shore, and elsewhere probably too, and it is most pleasant to find them quietly pouring out their bounty.

Now the snow falling is very fine, and with no wind it is almost like a haze dropping dreamily, an adumbration, never touching down, just dropping dreamily and softly. The tree tops across the river touch the clouds and poke their tops into the haze of snow-filled low skies.

The hills to the south are shrouded and disappear behind the screen of white, slow, snow falling. The snow doesn't seem to fall, but simply disengages and continues from the clouds. There is no separation between cloud and snow. Sounds do not exist for a while. The world here is silent, with barely falling snow painting white the woods.

This visual and auditory calm, this dimming, enhances the variety of winter, often thought to be dull and boring, but really full of subtle differences and even tastes of a beauty both gentle and fierce, both calm and frenetic. Another facet of beauty.

This time is a time of moods, of rapid changes and longer drawn-out elements of sameness. It is a cold month that hints of spring with a few days of thaw and the smell of wet wood. The other seasons do the same, or rather we find in them, and notice in them, these foreshadowings of changes and of nostalgic images. These foreshadowings are part of our view of nature, and nature's senses, like the foreshadowings that touch our lives in general. Sometimes these foreshadowings rise from the essence of us, of our depths. They too are often muted and unclear like the hills and the trees under a soft falling snow. They hint to us of secrets and mysteries of which we are a part. Silent speeches of the soul, beyond the haze of falling snow.

As winter moves on, the ice on the river, softening in the middle during the thaw of the past few weeks, and affected by the movement of the water beneath it, has changed to a dark mottled color. The wind has swept it clear of snow, except along the shores, and of course, much of the snow in the center has been devoured by the water seeping through and over the ice in that area. For a few days the river middle looks like the spring thaw, but we have time to go in winter. There will be more freezes and heavy snows into this winter/spring.

Today the cold has come again. Accompanied by sharp flurries of snow, the river wet spots have frozen solid, even in the current warm middle. Along the shore, of course, the ice has remained fresh and solid, except above the springs, pumping their fresh and warmer water up into the river.

On the shore lines the brush stands bare and clawlike, the deciduous trees sentinels with every arm exposed, clattering in the wind, and the evergreens, tall white pines, spruces, and balsams, as well as the cedars and hemlocks, darker green than in the summer, all braving the ripping wind roaring out of the northern skies.

In those protective evergreens, the chickadees and juncos and siskens and jays live. The other day we saw American goldfinches by the feeder, earlier than usual, flashes of gold flickering over and under the deck and into the trees. The birds are active and interesting, colorful and bright, and provide a look of busy life out in the cold winter environment.

In the forest the heavy balsam growth northwest of the house is coated with snow, and the bright sun gleams off the white. The contrast of dark green balsam and white snow is striking. We see it every winter. It is still striking. Up high the wind is heard in the upper reaches of the trees, and the tops of the trees bend, and the wind howls and whistles up there. Down here among the thick growth, among the many tracks of deer and rabbits and squirrels, it is calm. The places the sun strikes are very warm, and it is silent. To break off a few balsam fir needles is to fill the air momentarily with the happy, pungent smell of Christmas trees. And the needles will hold that pleasant odor for a long time.

The snow is surprisingly deep here, despite the warm weather, but that may be due to the heavy shade in this area.

The walk home is a tough one, given the deep snow, lack of snowshoes, and heavy young balsam growth. The steepness of the hillside increases the difficulty of an already hard walk. We, my wife and I, follow a set of deer tracks to the east, and soon come out in the clearing south of the house that looks out over the river. The sun is warm on our faces, and here, occasional whips of wind, cold wind, touch us. It is pleasant and fresh and cold, and the smell of balsam fir is on our hands and in the air. It is a sunny late winter afternoon.

In the clear sky to the south I can see a speck, possibly an eagle, but as it grows larger it becomes two ravens, circling, diving, and turning close to each other as though it were spring. During their mating they fly together, often quite as high as a couple of thousand feet, and gyrate and roll and almost seem to play. Today they act almost the same way. Staying close to each other, they perform aerobatics to envy any pilot, especially in the formation they hold and change constantly. The wind drifts them over the house, and off to the south again, I see two more dancing together in the crisp blue. The crows do this sort of thing also, but I don't think on as grand an altitude scale as their cousins, these ravens. But the crows are playful. Often as they fly along in a loose flock, several will roll and play and harass each other. Perhaps it's something else, but it does appear playful.

Eagles also, when they mate, will climb high and dive, turning together until they drop to several hundred feet. But these ravens behave almost as if it were spring. Perhaps we expect them only to do things when we have ascertained they should be done. Whatever the case, it was delightful to see the ravens dance. It reminded me of the coming spring.

Again, the morning shows the woods frosted over, pure sparkling shining white on the branches of the trees. The pines look a muted green, iced with frost. A fog early in the morning, probably due to a temperature inversion, caused this. On another scale the First Cause caused it. You can shake it off the trees later in the morning when the sun loosens it, and you can brush it off cold now in the early morning.

We are part of nature in one sense, but we are able to control nature in another. The paper on which this is written was once part of a tree, on which frost formed on a foggy winter morning. We can use it profitably. We can still be stewards. We are able to use the forces and resources of nature even though we are part of nature—that is, we are created. The beauty of the frost on the trees, gleaming against the early blue sky, is a beauty, a gift. But it hasn't made itself. The beauty of the Creator is awesomely reflected in the things we are given. The beauty of humans is even more marvelous, but we haven't made ourselves either. And we do make magnificent things, great art and architecture and engineering and scientific marvels. They are good and they can serve us. We have power over them unless we surrender to materialism, and we have power over the other created things. Beauty reflects the Creator, and the beauty of our Creator is illimitable and is given and shown to us. For us. An idea of the abstract, the transcendental, and the ability to choose and use for our benefit, the created gifts, speaks against a purely biological nature grown within itself. This awareness speaks of the beyond. It was G. K. Chesterton who pointed out that if you take the supernatural out of nature, all you have left is the unnatural.

The frost slowly disappears in the warming sun. The laws of nature. We use them too: airplanes fly, woods are turned to paper, the laws of thermodynamics, of chemistry, of mathematics, of logic. Far beyond that, above the formal logic, but connected to it, is faith and love. There is more beauty in the Creator, as beautiful as this creation is. Our awareness grows like the frost which simply seems to appear, despite our awareness of the laws of physics and chemistry that explain how it occurs. These "laws" did not simply create themselves either. They are the outpouring of creation, Christmas and Easter.

This morning, again, is one of those which has deposited on every limb of every tree, every twig, and every branch, a hoary pure white coating of frost. Walking slowly through the woods toward the east, I can see tiny sparkling flakes of frost fall, and when the imperceptible breeze moves, the flakes of glittering frost stop their slow fall and move horizontally, or even vertically momentarily, before resuming their gentle, soft drop to the earth.

The trees are all white and glittering, and now with this breeze, the frost falls and climbs and turns and finally drops to the ground, in minute crystals that reflect the dim, cloud-hidden sun every second.

The sky today is clouded, pearly bright against occasional openings of blue, pale also because of the thin veil of cloud. The cloud edges are indistinct, indicating that they are made up of crystals, ice crystals. The very crisply distinct edges of clouds of summer are usually an indication that they are made up of water, in the form of droplets or water vapor. These, today, are typical winter clouds, layering aloft, and in the west on the horizon is a dark blue line, the clouds of tonight that will bring snow. The deep, hard, cold snow of late winter. Yet the days are getting longer, very slightly, but longer, and this affects the weather. In not too long a time, it will be spring. Now the clouds move in slowly, and in an almost measured manner, drop cloudlets of quiet snow onto the woods. It looks like cold and snow tonight.

This beauty, even in the frigid cold of winter, does not reflect an altruism. There really is no altruism in the nature around us. Even the lovely and friendly chickadees fight for a place at the feeder.

Altruism is something above nature, something above man's animal nature. It must come from above, as must the movement toward civilization. Civilization does not, or should not, ignore nature. It really cannot, but it must refine those elements above nature—the values and virtues that are part of the qualities beyond nature. Nature itself does not produce a Mother Teresa, does not determine heroic, transcendental, or spiritual qualities. Not too long ago, T. H. Huxley, scientist and philosopher, indicated that man's goodness overshadows and contravenes nature's assumed direction.

Life would be unilluminated slavery if it were not in any way above nature. We see a beauty in nature. We also see violence, the prey-predator relationship. True Beauty is the source of nature and is greater than it. We have some of that greater quality, perhaps not a great deal, but it is there.

The clouds far out to the west are building dark inexorably. It will snow lovely clean white snow tonight, and instead of simply being covered thickly with it, we will watch and marvel about how and why it falls.

There certainly will be snow tonight. Inquisitiveness pleasantly anticipates it.

The snow began about midnight, and out on the deck a few minute cold flakes touched my face, frigid kisses indeed, but not meant to be anything else. They presaged the gentle fall of quiet snow later on, as we slept, and in the morning about an inch of silence lay about. If silence were to be materialized, one of its concrete manifestations might be a gentle snow. Motion in silence as all motion really is usually.

The snow fell more heavily during the day, furiously at times, obliterating the sky and trees and obscuring vision almost totally. White blindfold, different from the passive fog, yet as blinding. By late afternoon a foot had fallen, weighing the balsam and spruce and hemlock, coating the pines and the branches of deciduous trees.

Then the wind began to blow. I snowshoed to the mailbox and watched the wind knock clouds of snow off tree tops and whip and whistle the boughs and branches. The sky melded from plain vanilla gray, to very pale blue, and changed and grew to bright winter cold blue, with a few furry-edged clouds spewing clusters of snow low to the tree tops.

Before dark several pine grossbeaks, their ruby red shockingly beautiful against the snow, visited the feeder on the deck. Usually, we see evening grossbeaks, colorful in gold and gray, and of course the pine siskens, chickadees, nuthatches, American goldfinches, and occasional downy and hairy woodpeckers. These are visitors from farther north. The slatecolored juncos have not been around much, but the crows and ravens visit daily, visual and aural reminders of the familiar and common, and yet friendliest company.

The wind bursts along, whistling now and baring trees of their white. The few fast moving low, pale, bright clouds hurl fistfuls of snow flurries and pass on. The night will be clear, windy, and cold. Late winter in the north woods.

Tonight about 10:30 I saw a dark shape in the backyard beyond the deck. It was moving slowly, and the moon was not up. After some staring and visual gymnastics, including looking slightly to the side of the object (a method that helps you to see a specific thing in the dark), I turned the deck lights on. Outside was a large porcupine chewing peacefully on a piece of fish I had thrown out. It became a bit nervous after a while, so I turned the lights out. Then the porcupine, a rather large one, ambled off into the woods, somewhat in a hurry, but obviously trying to look dignified and beyond it all.

This bright cold and clear morning brings the sharp whiteness of winter into the fore again. After the snow yesterday, and 20 degrees below zero last night, the air is clear and visibility terrific. The snow is so bright it does hurt the eyes to look toward the sun over it.

A gentle wind blows easily among the tall pine tops but cuts the face sharply, razor-like stabs and slashes, when walking into it. My beard and mustache are quickly covered with frost when I walk in the woods in such weather. Then it is a special blessing to come into the house and unchill by the fireplace while looking out into the white cold outdoors, backed by the special blue of the cold winter skies.

An eagle is back. Today against the bright deep blue sky, a bald eagle flew down the trail about 30 feet above me. The dark feathers offset, in remarkable contrast, the bright white of his head and tail, which almost glistened in the sunlight. The eagle rowed gently away over the trees to the south. This may be a bit early for the eagles to return north, although this one may have wintered here, feeding around the open waters of the dams or the fast rapids of the river. Most of the eagles move south when the river freezes completely, as do the ospreys, which leave a lot earlier. If this is a "returnee," spring can't be too far from now.

Another sign of imminent spring is the smell of skunk. Whenever there is a smell of skunk odor in later winter, I think of upcoming spring. The skunks, partially hibernating or deep-sleeping much of the winter, do rise and move about on warm sunny days, as do the squirrels and some other winter sleepers. So the odor of a skunk, from a distance of course, is a nostalgic sign of spring not too far away, although we are coming into March, where the snows fall heavily and thickly before the warmth of the sun brings spring.

The signs of spring appear now more often and are gone as suddenly—the faint smell of fresh earth on a sunny warm day with the snow melting enough to be great packing. The enthusiasm for making snowmen and forts and snowballs seems, however, to have been left back with the early winter snows of November and December.

This "packing" snow means it will soon melt, I think. There is another whole meaning here, a different symbol, a different set of criteria, and a different goal.

The sun is warmer than it was a month ago and helps unzip a jacket or pull off a scarf. Without a heavy wind on a sunny day, one goes without a hat or cap. The spring is coming. But not without a few heavy snowfalls that will pound the earth in a ferocious farewell of winter. They will not last long, the snows from these March storms, but they will be heavy. These winter receding storms are pleasant in another way. We know they forecast the coming of green spring, dark clear water in the river, and tiny flowers and buds and leaves. Of course, the temperatures will still be rather low, and the nights will be in the teens, and often lower, for a long time.

Yet the softening snow keeps telling about this spring. Today a skunk's tracks cross the yard. They are up and about a lot more these days of waning winter.

Another sign of spring, a sign of more than the revivication of life, is Ash Wednesday, the beginning of Lent, the time leading to the death that destroys death because death does not hold Him, who rises. And this time reflects the fact that we can, and must, discipline ourselves, our appetites, but the rest of nature cannot. We function on another plane, perceiving the beauty of nature, living in it, but as stewards living and aiming beyond it. These days are not sad despite the minor fasts we make, but are anticipatory, as we await the great celebration of Resurrection.

March is a transition month, Lent to Easter, dormancy to Resurrection. Part of this beauty is just that—the essence of it—the path to the Resurrection, the special awareness and acceptance of God, the Other, in our midst, fully in and among us. And we open or close ourselves to this ineffable and superabundant love.

The warmth is almost disingenuous, hiding in its snug pleasantness somewhere near the still frozen ground close to the surface. The top of the snow melts and softens, the frost lies low, literally.

Out to the west, on this sunny prespring day, are wisps of mare's tails, bright white and ephemeral against the horizon, the milk white, almost white, porcelain color of a coming storm. A March storm which brings snow and sleet and sometimes, when the warmth sneaks in, a delightful rain.

The mare's tails portend a change in weather in about 24 hours. The sun shines brightly, and we think of spring, and warming rains, and thunder.

The snow that now falls is wet and mushy and turns into sleet which is transformed soon into rain. Gentle and consistent rain. Not a big storm this time. And the snow melts.

A large area in the middle of the river is open. The ice has broken up and the black water shows silently. Floes of ice float downstream, some 30 or 40 feet long, contrasting their deteriorating whiteness with the calm dark of the river. They move smoothly and almost grandly toward their melting point, however far downstream that may be. The river will not freeze solidly again until next winter. The open water sings spring, as do so many other activities and signs. The remaining snow is crowned everywhere with clouds of fog rising a few feet above it with the warming air. And in the open meadows the snow is easily located by these cloudy signposts, indicating seasonal change is coming.

We still may get another snow storm, but this warming period can mean nothing but the end of winter.

Tonight the moon is very bright and full and partially defies the magnificent green aurora borealis streaking toward the center of the sky through the patches of ground fog.

It is so bright I can easily read my watch, and on the deck the silence is palpably springish, with the smell of wet and fog and melting snow, while the black open river water gleams in the moonlight.

From the river a goose honks, a lone goose, calling to the night. Soon it will have much company, but now it, probably a local goose that stays all winter in the open water areas, calls in the night. Its honks echo down the river and off the hills, not quite plaintive, but lonely nevertheless. It must know spring is near.

Tonight is as dark as last night was bright. Dark, thick clouds cover the skies and fog hangs imperviously along the woods and roads and down to the river. The trees are only vague and nebulous shapes, and the river is not visible from the house. From the deck I can see only a few feet beyond, except for indistinct shapes.

Lightning flashes to the south, the light refracted over the whole fogged and clouded sky. Forty seconds later a throbbing rumble, not loud, but unmistakable, signals thunder. About eight miles away. The first thunderstorm of spring. I watch carefully to see the next flash of lightning, sometimes barely distinct, but welcome as the preparatory element to spring.

The rain begins its "pit-pat" on the roof. Soft and gentle. Later it will really rain, but this is a gentle spring rinsing away of the winter, of the dry, of the cold, of the snow. Spring is not far.

The fog molds around the hills and glides down the valleys, until it is a solid mass joined with the low clouds lighted by the lightning refracted from above.

Spring calls out its arrival, both day and night. The wind howls and pushes clouds north in bursts of energy, the energy of coming warmth.

The air is somewhat cooler today, and the gentle warmth of yesterday is gone, but still the realization of spring is here. This pause of movement, this reversion to a mild cooling is but temporary, is but a minor halt, perhaps to remind us that not too long ago the grip of winter held fast.

The return of mild warm weather will be doubly appreciated now. In the meantime the wind moves tree tops and branches, whips the few bits of litter of twigs, and decorates leaves about in an almost pathetic empty woods. But it is a warming wind. Behind it are warm and rainy skies, greening grasses and trees and weeds and flowers blooming. March winds here mean coming growth.

Today the world has become again a monochrome study,

black and white, or more accurately, dark and white, with tinges of green. The fickle season brought two inches of snow last night that covered every exposed twig and branch and needle.

The sky is filled with the gentle snow, and white is predominate everywhere. The road is perfectly clear except for the marks of deer and squirrel and a few rabbits. Black and white everywhere, with the dark green evergreens of late winter touching color into the picture.

March snow, delaying spring, perhaps providing more moisture for it. The monochromatic familiarity of winter snow is back, but only for a short time. The warming is inevitable.

Two marsh hawks, harriers, startlingly bright, the whitish male, and beige and white female, soared 10 feet above me while I walked in the field at the end of our road. They were terrific in their gentle soaring movements, crossing over one another and gliding, turning gracefully. This is the first time I've ever seen marsh hawks together. Often we've seen them hunt individually, working the fence lines and the fields, hunting mice, but always one or the other. Now in spring they are together, perhaps to mate and soon lay eggs.

The predators usually bear their young sooner than the socalled nonpredators. This probably ensures their survival to some extent. These marsh hawks are stylishly attired, their whites, grays, and blacks offset by the beiges: bars and stripes and little knicks of color, beautiful and graceful birds with their pointed wing tips, hunting low to the ground in undulating flight.

SPRING

A ROBIN HOPS along the road ahead of me. Spring is here. Fat-looking, he or she is fluffed up in the upper 20s F cold and busily works the edge of the road. The marsh hawks won't see him here, but a Cooper's or goshawk may. Still, he's quite safe and busy feeding on whatever insect is now available or seeds and other vegetation. It won't be long now before the summer birds begin to arrive and the more dormant animals begin to awaken.

Last night in a fog on the river, its eyes probably searching through the trees on the bank, a great horned owl called. Its eerie call, a shriek almost, opposed to the gentle usual hoot, echoed along the river. The night was a hunting night surely. Everything was fog and quiet except for the owl, which was quiet too, later.

On the ice at the edge of the river, a bit of thawing ice left, five crows peck to get a piece of frozen fish, gripped by the ice last fall as it floated dead on the surface. The next look brings me the five crows as before, but with the addition of a bald eagle, majestically larger than the crows, its dark body crowned with the white head. It too wanted some of the fish. The birds worked industriously at chipping away the ice until they finally reached their meal, squabbling a bit but all apparently eating, including the eagle, which deigned to sup with the lively crows. Later, above the house in the clear sky, two crows wheeled and turned with each other, one always closing, until they made contact. Immediately one turned away, banked sharply in a tight turn, and repeated the performance of mating with the other. It was a graceful display, the dark birds turning and banking, sometimes 90-degree banks, and finally meeting again, this time for a longer period, to separate and wheel the sky around again.

Then the birds drifted off to the north, still circling and dancing against the blue, occasionally calling until the sky was alone.

The warming air and the sun shining are making a subtle but evident change in the woods. The evergreens, which had become a dull dark green at the end of winter, are brighter, vitally brighter, everywhere in the woods. And the buds of the deciduous trees are elongated and full, some glistening with the pregnant hope of birth beneath their hard shells.

The river gleams black in the morning sun, a very occasional ice floe, small and rotten, passing by, and the birch across the river also gleam, like freshly glazed and painted pillars of some atavistic temple. But they are, I suppose, pillars of a sort and do reflect the handwork of the Creator.

The air is slightly wet and the earth smell is stronger these days. The day too is much longer, and the sun warms and speeds the beat of rhythm that turns to spring.

The two local geese fly patterns in formation, calling and calling, probably for the many geese preparing to fly up from their southern winters. Soon they will sound their calls all through the area, as will the ducks and countless other birds. The juncos, those hardy slate black and white friends, are moving back north to summer in the far reaches of Hudson Bay and the tundra country.

More birds appear daily and the evening grossbeaks flock to the feeder. It is becoming a busy time. The killdeer too are back, running quickly and calling shrilly in quick-tempo "cheeps." They move around open grassy areas in formallooking attire. They are handsome and joyful appearing birds, moving in a quick step, a controlled run, stopping to eat something from the grass, and then continuing.

The adults are great at mimicking a broken wing when one approaches their eggs or young, the latter tremendously well camouflaged. They are like balls of dun-colored fluff, and they are capable of lying perfectly still until danger passes, with an assist from the adults pretending to have broken wings, and dragging a leg, and fluttering, feigning injury. These birds certainly signal spring, as do the robins that appeared a few days ago.

The snow is almost gone. Today the sun shone brightly from a clear sky and the only places it could not touch were the northerly slopes of ridges and hills and gullies. Along the road a three-foot ridge line of old snow forms a short barrier, and today there still is dingy snow lying several inches deep in the shade.

Under the dirt and grime, though, the snow is pure white, like when it fell. It is granular and crystalline, as opposed to the softness that fell. Soon that snow will melt too, and the green of summer will reappear. The verdant rich softness of summer growth, belying its strength and power, begins to move.

A resurrection is occurring in time with the celebration of the ultimate Resurrection. The timing of the parallel is no accident. The Mideast has its spring now too. Of course, the southern hemisphere has autumn during Easter, but the season doesn't matter: we will be renewed. All things will be renewed, in a permanent manner.

Grouse are booming in the woods north of the house. The deep soft sounds began slowly, increased in intensity and rapidity, and ended as a drum roll fading away. This mating rite of the ruffed grouse is wonderful to hear and is caused, as mentioned earlier, by the male beating his wings so tiny sonic booms are created as the air moves past the wing feathers.

The grouse likes to stay near or on a fallen log or stump, and supposedly grouse return to the same drumming logs each year.

The male entices females to his area this way. A unique mating ritual and one that reflects the mystique of the north woods.

The sound is so deep it almost, if you are not aware of it at first, seems to be coming from your own head or chest. It is a mellifluous throb which obviously hastens the heart beat of the grouse as well as that of the north woods aficionado, and any student of nature. As Gerard Manley Hopkins points out in his poetry, the variety of nature speaks awesomely of God.

The chipmunks are awake also. Two very lively and hungry chipmunks competed with the gray and pine squirrels for seeds below the deck. The chipmunks filled their cheek pouches full to the point they looked incongruous, rushing to the woods with heads held low, cheeks bulging.

This must be a great windfall to them, these seeds.

A black (gray) squirrel has been on and under the deck often this past week. It is a beautiful squirrel and somewhat uncommon, but not as rare certainly as are albino squirrels. Its color does not seem to affect its relationships with the others.

The night was cool and some little evidence remains in the morning that snow flurried to the ground. A few white areas in the grass attested to winter's slow yielding grip. The sun rose in a clear sky, and the air warmed rapidly. The whole day was clear and bright and warming. The birds were especially active at the feeder on the deck, and over the river several groups of ducks moved regularly, not in the numbers or frequency of early summer, but it was evident that many waterfowl are beginning to return to the North.

After Mass we returned with our blessed palms and took down the old ones and burned them in the fireplace, a tradition which in its simplicity was very pleasant and signaled Holy Week, spring, and most important, Resurrection. Then we placed the new palms in their special places. There are many special places in the house, and in the woods too, but some special places exist in the self, in the soul, open to contemplation of everything leading to God. There is a blending, an amalgamation, of contemplating reality that leads to the contemplation of the Creator, God, whose love creates the world, enters it as Christ, the Word, and in the ultimate act of self-abnegation, love, and humility, offers Himself and rises, salving us and renewing all. And that is why, amidst the great creation there must be, as Edith Stein, St. Teresa Benedicta of the Cross says, special created places in which to pray. Created by us for the Creator.

The ultimate contemplation occurs when the soul opens itself to the contemplation of God's mind. This is the highest freedom. This is the highest necessity.

In the early evening the breeze calmed and the surface of the river stilled, like the contemplation of the day. A lone call of a loon sang through the air. A loon was back. One loon at least, perhaps the same one I saw off the cove last fall. It was a wonderful call. Another very special sound of the north woods.

The moon rose bright late that evening. In the southwest a bank of clouds appeared quietly and without pretension. Perhaps it would rain tonight. Rain on the ducks and the loon and the trees and the slightly greening grasses, and on the roof to make a rhythmic sound for sleeping gently. On the road and earth and rocks and springs and river to trickle everywhere and dampen and freshen and rejuvenate. Like spring. Like Resurrection.

The first raccoon we've seen this year climbed up on the deck and strolled casually about, looking for sunflower seeds lying about from the bird feeder. It was a young one, perhaps a couple of years old at most, and when it realized I was watching through the patio doors, it looked at me with its masked eyes, then put down its head, and very gently, almost as though tiptoeing, moved across the deck and climbed down the side of the house. The coon looked almost as though it had been shamed.

We look forward to seeing it, or others, again. They are such clever animals, and when a group of youngsters are playing, they make a rather humorous sight with their leaping and playing antics, their terrific agility, and quite handsome looks.

This morning the breakfast presentation was two yearling white tail deer just fifteen feet from the kitchen window, and after they finished their casual browsing in the yard, an argument that became a battle, and then simply an argument again, by two male ruffed grouse. We noticed them after the deer had left, as a flurry of wings, tails, and feathers punctuated by both combatants facing each other and dodging, feinting, and ducking. Both also tried to stretch themselves to look taller, but the one that won this contest invariably exposed so much of himself he was quickly attacked by the shorter one. This contest took place on the slope in the back, as mentioned, in front of the window. The weeds are down and matted from the snow, so the grouse were readily visible.

After several furious wing-flapping attacks, they continued their face-off, but gradually one stepped back a step or two every few minutes. When pushed too hard during these subtle retreats, he reacted vigorously, but was apparently trying to get away without turning his back and ingloriously fleeing. He finally reached the woods, turning occasionally to look back, and the victor watched him step away.

They will be mating throughout spring, and their booming will begin again as soon as the weather warms from this unseasonable chilliness.

The grouse probably were fighting over "booming" territory, and it will be interesting to see if the victorious male will boom right outside our kitchen window. We hope so. It will be another gift on top of all we have been given. One cannot help but somehow honor God.

Today we celebrate the greatest gift: Easter, the Resurrection. The incarnate Jesus Christ, overcoming the world and, at the same time, redeeming it. Redeeming us, and all creation.

The sky today is bright blue, and in the morning the sound of geese honking comes through the trees. As it grew louder, I ran to the yard and could see a skein of geese, continually wearing across the sky, maintaining a loose V heading north. Soon after the first group of about 70 Canada geese had passed, another, larger formation appeared on the horizon, like a wisp of smoke, a thread in the sky. This second group was well over 100, and they were holding an accurate V.

Groups of about this size passed steadily throughout this morning, some fairly high, others only a few hundred feet or so. Some of these geese would be stopping in our area, but many were heading into the great swamps and wetlands in Canada to mate and raise their young. The young must develop enough strength to be able to fly south again in the fall.

The sight of geese migrating, especially in spring, is an exciting one, mysterious in one sense, comfortably orderly and regular in another. Nature is certainly more than just touched by God. There are mysteries that we are driven to discover, and rightly so, and there are greater mysteries that cannot be simply resolved. Yet there is an awareness of the answer. Reality is a narrative, not a slogan, and has an apex, an apogee, a point at which all the narrative comes together, a coherent fulfillment in perfection. There is a beginning and an end in a syncopation in every aspect. There is in nature a visible, if one searches enough, and is open enough, eschatology that involves us totally, we humans especially. Despite the stabbing apparent disorder, there is a euphony, the melodic narrative that can overcome the Fall and is a hint of fulfillment in a perfect symphony. Of contemplation of the Truth.

Later, in the afternoon quiet, two bald eagles soared over the river and the house, probably the pair that are nesting in a tall pine on the river about a half mile away. They soared gracefully in the area and moved with the light breeze to the north. We will see them soon again, I'm sure.

Early this evening, several flights of ducks whizzed along the river. Many ducks have completed their migration and the local population is visible to a great degree. A pair of teal swam gently into the cove right up to shore and paddled around. They left soon after their exploration, swimming into the still bent and brown bulrushes left from the winter.

Not long after the teal swam away, a lone large bird circled up river, calling curiously. It drifted down closer to me by the cove. It wasn't a heron, because the neck stretched out, and it circled, almost like a hawk or eagle. As it neared almost overhead, I recognized a sandhill crane, which summer in this area to some extent. The crane was large, with broad wings, and now I could see the legs trailing behind. The bird called constantly, and finally drifted along down the river, flapping regularly and intermittently soaring.

Later, in the early twilight, squirrels chattered in the trees, and a grouse drummed in the woods, the booming sounds deep and solid, their deep reverberations increasing to a rattle and finally fading, the picture of a timpanist slowing contact with the drums until one strained to hear the muted, echoing thump. The image remained long after the sound faded. The image of a sound. A contemplative image.

As the light faded even more, a loon appeared on the river, floating gently, keeping station across from the cove against the gentle current. It didn't call, though I hoped it would, and instead, disappeared in a quiet swirl of water to appear a few seconds later in the reflection of birch from across the river.

The ripples livened the birch white reflections and pricked the sinking red sunset gleaming from between the trees.

The loon swam into the current and stayed in one place until the water calmed, and it became part of the reflections of white birches barring the water, with the sky in countless shades of magenta behind the trees.

Just before the loon and the birch disappeared in the darkening water, five ducks, mallards it appeared, winged over the surface of the river, their wings whistling in their typical way, turned, and approached together, in fine formation, to splash down in front of the cove. They paddled through their own landing ripples, which reflected now only the last fires of a blazing sunset, and headed into the cove.

The squirrels were quiet, the loon somewhere across the river silent, like the air. The ducks chuckled gently. In the west behind the trees, light faded to a glow. To the north the beginnings of the aurora borealis dimmed the big dipper and the north star in sporadic awakening. The air was crisp fresh, a tinge of crushed pine needles drifting across the cove.

Night had come, a calm covering toward rest for some, activity for others.

This morning, Oscar, as we've named one (or all) of the pine squirrels, has come to look in the patio door by the kitchen. It has become nosily unafraid of us and looks for hand-outs regularly. Oscar scurries along the deck as we prepare for Mass. The sun glows onto his red fur and lively tail. Oscar will feed on the sunflower seeds we throw on the deck and then wait for our return. The birds, among them purple finches, looking as though they had been dipped by the tails in raspberry juice, are enjoying the seeds this morning, along with a few gray squirrels below the deck.

When we return, the deck will be an active landing field for birds and a feeder for squirrels. Our mourning doves will be there too, almost always in pairs, cooing sometimes, usually silent, and feeding elegantly in their blue gray feathers and gentle movements. Their shapes are curve upon complex curve, the head and neck bowed on rounded body tapering to long tails. They too partake of the seeds, usually pecking at the dropped bits below the deck.

After they feed, they will fly to the pines by the house and coo softly, singing a quiet morning song.

Another spring arrival is the yellow-shafted finch, a large handsome bird with a powerful striking beak, and a bright orange red spot on the back of the head, as well as a black half moon on the breast. It is an active woodpecker type bird that has strong, wide wings and calls loudly in a "yuk" sound that certainly heralds spring.

This evening, with a calm clear sky and the temperature in the 50s, I heard the sound that so thoroughly means spring in the north woods: the peepers singing. These little pale greenbrown tree frogs sing and harmonize beautifully in the night and present a melodious background to the woods in the dark. They are small frogs with pads on the tips of their fingers that allow them to stay wherever they decide, even on glass and upside down. Very handsome, for frogs I suppose. They are great insectivores and pleasant sounding, too. In the summer they do not sing at night as their peeping call is probably a mating call used in the spring. Of course, this is the early symphony. In the coming warmer weather, the woods near the river and the swamps will reverberate with the concert overtures of the peepers. A delightful, nostalgic, pleasant, and melodious sound of the north.

This evening also is a climax for the whole day's flights of geese, which came, wave after wave, unraveling and reraveling skeins, honking overhead to the north. At one time I could see over a thousand geese in seven or eight flights, the V formations changing and weaving. These were moving toward the northwest, perhaps to several of the lakes in that direction.

In between these grand flights was the gentle peeping of the peepers, perhaps preparing for their later choruses in the dark.

On the river the loon, which has apparently taken a liking to the area near the cove, appeared suddenly behind some dry bulrushes. It saw me first, and its head was visible, like a periscope on a submarine. Then it dove, dipping its head and disappearing under water. I did not see it resurface but saw a disturbance on the water about 100 yards up- stream.

The geese continued to fly over, in an uncountable number of formations, a variety of patterns and skeins of birds in the sky. Gerard Manley Hopkins, in his poem, "Pied Beauty," describes the endless beauty and diversity of creatures functioning for their Creator. Here it is!

Two of the local geese flew back and forth along the river calling to the traveling geese, and on two occasions joined up with flocks and appeared to entice them to land. After several unsuccessful tries, they joined a small flight and landed together a couple of hundred yards upstream from the cove.

The sky has been blue, with clouds moving from the south all day, a tailwind for the migrators, and now as the sun sets, only the highest cirrus clouds form soft white fans at stratospheric heights.

The geese keep coming. Some in small groups of 40 or 50, most in large flights weaving and pounding their way across the sky, sometimes in almost perfect Vs, usually forming varieties of lines right above the river.

A muskrat broke my concentration on the sky for a moment, and swam into a burrow along the north bank of the cove I hadn't noticed before. A few minutes later it entered the cove from another burrow, saw me, and dove hurriedly.

The sun is almost set, and the geese have stopped arriving. But they will probably continue tonight, a navigational wonder explicable simply—the Creator's will. Secondarily explicable by the studies of light, stars, magnetism, and so on. Either way, one wonder of life, one gift, one sense of awe. "Nature leads to grace," Aquinas said, so "Let All the Earth Cry out with Joy to the Lord," as the psalmist tells us, and tells us, and tells us.

With just a faint glow of light in the west and the peepers joyfully singing their simple but inimitable chorus, the sound of northering geese still sounded across the river. Out of the dark in the south they flew overhead, and I could only get a faint sense of movement against the edges of the night sky.

I did catch sight of another migratory creature, the bat, who flew against the light portion of the sky 30 feet from my post on the deck. The bats migrate enormous distances, like the geese and ducks and other birds, but most of their flights are at night and, some say, at rather high altitudes. Whatever the case, the bats being back fills another element, previously missing, in the activity of the spring north woods.

The bat made several more passes visible to me while the peepers sang happily and the geese familiarly called out their arrival home, until the night became too dark to see through and urged me to sleep.

Very early in the morning, in the very dark before the dawn, again the sound of distant geese reached out. They were still coming. During breakfast we saw flight after flight, and now, at noon on a cloudy warm day, they still fly over in waves, weaving and floating across the sky, never losing touch with some relationship, stretched out toward their goal. Occasionally, one can see a snow goose or blue goose with the Canadas, fitted into a spot in the formation.

Once in a while also, when the flocks are low, a few geese will set their wings and drop down to see what's on the water, perhaps to land.

The sky is filled with sound and life and wings. The sky is filled with spring.

Warm and gentle rain falls, the pleasant dampness of spring rain, but on the horizon are darker clouds that light up when lightning creases through them. They are coming toward us.

That will be a more ferocious rain, one that slants down hard, and roars against the woods, driven by gusts of wind and flashed by lightning. The tender rain began early this morning after a few large cumulus buildups yesterday afternoon.

It is badly needed, this rain, since several years of dryness and a rather dry spring so far need amelioration. Everything is freshened by this spring rain: the grasses are greening, bushes budding, even the aspen groves are topped by an airy fluff of pale green, the buds opening into tiny leaves.

On the road to the mailbox are occasional catkins, the furry-looking seed holders of many trees, but here the birch. Some birches are pregnantly heavy with the catkins hanging from the top of every branch, every twig and stub of twig that will have a leaf.

Through the soft rain this morning came several more flocks of geese, honking low over the woods across the river, keeping a close formation in the V, not far from their destination now. They are beautiful in the rain too and cosignatories of spring with the rain.

We see only the arrivals and do not see those who were not able to make it this far. Not many fell, or stopped, of course, but nature is ordered, not necessarily orderly. Nature is not God and is not to be worshiped. It certainly manifests direction and reflects order, and its beauty is a minuscule, and infinitesimal, touch of God's love: else why would we find something like beauty?

The philosophical moment rises to the questions that arise in seeing nature—questions with answers profounder than nature—beyond it.

But nature does lead to grace. The geese flying through the tactile rain over the river in the spring do not attest to it, but the questions and awe and beauty they reflect attest to it. That beauty does not exist for itself; it exists for the God who created it and the humans who perceive it. We have the freedom to observe and develop concepts, the freedom to contemplate beauty. It distinguishes us from all else in nature, no matter how beautiful, in a special paean to beauty and truth.

It becomes evident that people do not exist for the earth and nature. The earth and nature exist for humans who are a part of it, yet transcend it. A great absurdity it is to place human beings on the same level as other elements of nature. It is a blindness, a prejudice, against not only humans but against the God of nature and God the Creator. For God is not elusive. We elude Him, though, when we ignore the inherent awareness of Him in reality and close ourselves to it.

The storm comes, no longer the placid rain, but the flashing downpour that soaks the ground and creates rivulets around the trees. It is a short storm and suddenly ends, in bursts of rain and lightning and thunder, and dissipates into moistness.

After the rain stops, the fog hangs over the river in wisps of "ghost's breath," and the water calms in the quiet air. Nothing moves, as the earth and plants soak in the freshness of rain water. The blooms and leaves will soon react to this moisture, and the forest floor will move in a thousand different ways, animal and vegetable, in response to this rain.

The analogy of grace to rain as used by many contemplatives and saints, such as St. Teresa of Avila, is not tenuous or nebulous. They know the physical reality of rain and its effects. They also know the spiritual reality of grace and its effects.

Sunday morning after Mass and breakfast, the deck is warm and comfortable. The temperature is in the low 60s and the air calm. Everything is becoming luxuriously green, still the fresh bright spring green, but vibrant and verdant, with promise of lush summer greenness.

The few clouds are brushmark mild against blue summerish sky. The next level down are some high stratus, milky still under the cirrus brushes, and mostly blue sky above. Barely any wind exists.

I can hear many sounds from the woods. Several types of birds calling or making sounds like wood-pecking, the crows obviously with their officious cawing, the ravens subtle, the jays imperious and excited, others I cannot identify but are still familiar.

A raven flies by the house, high, almost over the river in a long gentle gliding turn toward the woods. Going in the opposite direction, down river and a hundred feet higher, a bald eagle floats calmly, just a twitch of wings giving away the existence of other than perfect calm and gently rising thermals upon which the eagle and the raven soar.

The sun is warm on the deck and on my back. The river reflects it in its enjoyable motion, not always visible, but there.

There is a peacefulness here in the sun. An activity, yet a peacefulness. To the creatures around me, though, it is a matter of simply going about their designated functions, not spectacular or singular, not quotidian, just fulfilling something not only assigned but inherently directed.

Green is a multiplicity of colors. The woods now, after unseasonably warm weather, have turned shades of green of every level. The buds barely opening present a secret delicate green that almost glows. It is almost a blanched green but contrarily is full of life. It is vibrant, pale green. The leaves in stages of development all reflect a different green, and still not maturing leaves still another green. The hills to the south are brushed airily with the tender green of thousands, no, millions, of buds slowly and silently exploding, a visual song. A slow motion bomb. The contrast between the deep greens of the pines, spruces, balsams, and cedars contrasts with the soft green of the very early deciduous leaves. Of course, the evergreens will soon have delicate pale green tips from their new growth, but that will add another patina of special green to the scene.

The tamarack (or larch) in the swamps turned gold not too long ago and now are green as they begin to revitalize. Bushes too are becoming verdant and lively, and very soon the visibility in the woods will be quite limited by the verdure of vibrantly shaded multitoned greens, from hard to soft colorings, from almost pale to almost black, greens of spring, greens of summer.

This morning I saw a large red-tailed hawk in the top of a dead birch just 100 feet from the house. He sat for a while, turned, and flew about 50 feet to another tree and began to set down on a limb. On the limb was another hawk, and the first settled on its back for a few seconds, then flew a few feet, and perched on a limb.

Thus began a new spring for the hawks and their progeny. The other birds in the area are also preparing to nest, and in another month or so young birds will begin to appear.

While eating supper and enjoying the vivacious greens of new growth on the trees toward the river and across it, I noticed some movement in the woods to the right and below the house. The movement resolved itself into a bear, a glossy black bear, probably around 300 pounds, which strolled out of the woods up the hill toward the house, toward us. It stopped, obviously seeing us through the large window in the dining area. When my wife called for my daughter, the bear, which had been still for several seconds became nervous and rambled (that seems to be the only way to describe the movement) away to the open area between the river and the house. It moved fairly quickly, looking back once or twice toward us.

The whole scene was great. Great to see this marvelous animal so close to our house and us. It was glossy, almost blue black, quite healthy looking, its brown muzzle pointing toward the house accepting scents.

We sat at the table a while after the bear disappeared into the woods, pleased to have been able to see this interesting creature that had, not over two months ago, been asleep in a marvelous way, hibernating over the winter. More wonder. More awe. Yet not even the greatest by far.

The spring is evident in the birds too, particularly the predators. The hawks, owls, ospreys, and other predatory birds nest earlier than the others, as do, it appears, other types of predators. Probably this ensures food for their young.

It is seemingly cruel, yet it is the order of apparent disorder, the resulting order of a Fall affecting all creation. Cause and effect are visible here. Function toward an end, an end that is the function, is irrational, as though a conclusion were exactly the same as its premises. The argument in support of solely biological existence contradicts itself because the argument itself is beyond the purely biological. In fact, simply to think of more than the biological possibilities directs itself to more than the biological.

As St. Paul says, despite corruption of man and nature, the world itself will share in redemption and future glory, through the incarnation of the ineffable Word.

Mysteries of nature exist. Mysteries of immutable things exist. The Creator, by definition, allows mysteries to exist for us. We are not gods, but we are promised the opportunity to be with God, the End, the Fulfillment. And when we contemplate, see, view, become aware, open ourselves to the Creator, silently pray, God touches us. Contemplatives like St. Teresa of Avila and St. John of the Cross knew that. They, and others like St. Therese of Lisieux, sought truth, and in their honesty and humility, were able to contemplate deeply. As Aristotle said, the deepest desire of humans is to know, to contemplate. And the ultimate contemplation is of God.

The morning sky against which the hawks flew is blue. All day it remained bright blue. I think I know why it is blue. Really, I know how it is blue, but I don't know why.

Swallows are sitting on the wire by the road, dark against the lighter sky, having suddenly appeared from their southern visit. They, barn swallows, rough-winged swallows, tree swallows, and cliff swallows, swoop and curve the sky in their flights after insects. Magnificent flyers, they are so agile and aerobatic that it is pure joy to watch them, that inherent aerobatic ability, awesome.

Their pointed wings and streamlined shapes are attractive, and of course efficient for the flying they do. Once I saw the parents and five young swallows, just out of the nest a few days (the nest was under the eaves of our house), play follow the leader in a series of aerobatics that were amazing. It appeared to be a training session for the young, but that may have been appearance only. It was delightful flying, certainly.

Two robins have been visiting the front yard every morning. They, perennial spring signatures, are so familiar they are casually passed off, but they are handsome birds that add a great deal to life in the area. A careful look at them reveals very interesting markings, such as the white line around the eyes.

They certainly represent the coming summer, and their cheerful and loud calls and songs are obvious to all who have tried to sleep a bit later than normal occasionally.

Another flying creature with an ameliorative reputation for destroying pests of man is the amazing dragonfly. Double sets of wings buzzing and rattling, it speeds forward, stops and hovers, backs up, rises and descends, all while searching and eating minute insects. What a guy! Or gal! Or whatever!

What we call the dragonfly is really one of several varieties of creatures, popularly called dragonflies, and they are harbingers of hot summer days and boats, and water and the small delicate blue damselfly, cousin to the dragonfly, sitting on the end of a fishing rod. Somnolently and warmly pleasant ideas and memories.

Half a dozen red-winged blackbirds flash their red shoulders as they perch on bulrushes and stalks in the swamp. Several lean forward and partially spread their wings, flashing the bright red shoulder patch, swelling it outward in an attempt to attract a mate.

The red, and often a bright yellow or white line bordering part of it, is extremely bright against the shiny black feathers. It is a most beautiful and interesting sight. Something that leads to a question of beauty and grace and order. But that is not the only reason nature leads to grace. It is the laws of nature, of physics as we know them, of man's complexity beyond other animals, of mankind's transcendent thrust, that leads to God, to the Creator. And that is a triumph. The knowing of the Creator, the contemplative act of awareness given.

It is the unanswered question as well as the answered ones that lead us to the realization that our dignity cannot come from us simply, but must come from that which is greater than us, the Creator.

Nature constitutes not just a sunset, or birds singing, or marvelous scenery. Nature constitutes the interweaving of these things with man. The environment is not just a river or lake ecology, it is that ecology in relation to man, who is not only part of it but beyond it. Nature constitutes the ineluctable relationships that exist between all mundane and mutable things, beauty, and the abstract elements and transcendent things, the soul, and the immutable and the infinite, the supernatural, the Creator. Nature is more than we can see and hear. There is that element of nature that is transcendent, that we can touch, or rather which touches us, when we truly are contemplative.

Contemplation is a loving attainment of awareness. It is intuition of the beloved object, says the philosopher Josef Pieper, and Montaigne adds, "without love there would be no contemplation." Thus, the source of love, Love itself, leads us to contemplate, to not disregard the intellect, but to be beyond even the intellect. Without love, dying before and for the other, suggests St. Paul, there is nothing.

And nature leads to grace then in the simplest way: that of awe in its beauty, as well as in the most complex and convoluted way, in the search through order that seems sometimes in disarray but ends in only awe. This also leads to grace, if we but allow it.

The morning is wet and green. A rain is falling gently, washing the leaves and buds and grass until they almost glow various shades of green, so bright they catch one's eyes and hold them, so clean and fresh in the quiet rain they vibrate life.

The rain is becoming mixed with occasional large snowflakes splatting on the grass and whacking the windows. It is cooling off and the snow increases. By early evening it is snowing wet flakes, and they are collecting on the ground and in the trees, giving the woods a pale green image. Thick snowfall accompanied by a strong wind brings in the night.

Several inches of snow, wet and thick, have accumulated overnight. The snow falls heavily, whipped by gusty winds. This May snowfall should not last but is amazing in its intensity, a last ferocious gasp of the winter we all thought was gone, destroyed totally by the 80-degree temperatures of a week ago.

While it roars snow past the windows, we know tomorrow or the next day will be wet and green and warming. Spring will return.

Meanwhile, the snow slows toward late afternoon, and by early evening the sky is clear and blue, the wind strong, and the world of the north woods in our area covered with snow eight to twelve inches deep. Unusual. Not extraordinary, though.

As the sun sets behind the big pines northwest of the house, a few thin clouds intone its pinkish rays onto the snow below the house near the river and bathe it, coat it, immerse it, in an awesomely gentle and lovely pink, the pink of a setting sun. The view is almost surrealistic, yet indubitably natural. The pink changes slightly to pale red magenta and the snow is dyed with this glow. On the trees where the snow is thick, on the boughs of pines where the snow weighs down, over the ground, the colors imitate themselves onto the snow. It is like the string section of a symphony playing, for a while, alone, or the flutes calling, or a bassoon solo against the calm of an orchestral caesura.

Twilight, and finally dark, erase these color poems, but they are replaced by the rising moon which shines like a spotlight onto the trees below the house, highlighting the hanging snow.

The sky is starred dimly because of the light of the moon. There are so many kinds of light: the analogies of lights and God are not accidental, surely.

The snow has melted and it again looks spring. The woods, which in winter are open and bared, and in summer, cloistered in green, are now still partly open, with only the bloom of fresh green in the way. Across the river that gentle bloom is beginning to hide the slope that leads to the river. Soon the deer, which leap from the road into the woods, will disappear entirely. Soon the bloom will again curtain the woods and the birch across the river.

Over the river, so low its wings tips caused tiny swirls in the calm spots, flew a great blue heron, long thin legs stretched behind, great wings slowly, even majestically, swinging in great half arcs to carry it along. This is the first heron I've seen this year and presages more. It also reminds of the warm summer evenings with the herons and egrets wading along the bulrushes and water lily pads, hunting very quietly until dark, then winging to their roosts against the darkening sky, only slow beating wings against the lighter sky and silhouettes of trees on the river.

I heard the raccoon climbing onto the deck while I sat in the dining room. Quickly, I turned out the lights and walked silently and slowly toward the patio door. Nothing. I flicked on the deck lights and walked to the living room patio door and there it was, the friendly raccoon of our meeting a few weeks ago. It looked like the same one anyway and was the same size. The coon strolled about the deck, dug into the flower pots, spread some of the earth around, and finally came to the patio door to look at my daughter and me looking at it.

Then, with a look of raccoon insufferable injury at its wasted effort, he or she strolled to the edge of the deck and climbed down.

The deer are all around the house this morning in the fog, strolling about, feeding casually, enjoying, it seems, the abundance of buds and browse available for them. They are almost a nuisance when you drive, but are interesting and handsome creatures and so part of the world we live in, and among, that here, in the north woods, and many other areas, an omission of deer would be shocking.

As the fog lifted the swallows appeared, a flock of about 30, diving and turning and climbing and maneuvering, even making hammerhead stalls out of steep climbs, where they fold their wings for a second, and stall and dive, re-extending their wings into another turn. Catching insects does certainly require precision flying. These swallows know how to do it, and they are magnificent to watch at their "trade."

The kestrels, or sparrow hawks, are back along the open meadows and fields, hovering before a strike onto a large insect or occasionally a mouse or meadow vole. They too are graceful at their work, as are most birds, most animals, and those we consider ungraceful have their own utility and beauty. Robinson Jeffers in "Boats in a Fog" reflects on the beauty of utility, but even within utility, and beyond utility, there is great beauty. Gerard Manley Hopkins reflects that in most of his poems. His perceptions are awe inspiring. Taken as they are from the essential elements of nature around us, the essence of those things, sources, from which beauty rises, they should be. There is his ability to apperceive, also, to contemplate, which is beauty in itself.

The rain had stopped late last night, and this morning the sun was poking out between broken clouds rolling from the west. The air was still cool, but there was a sense of warmth, more than a surreptitious awareness of spring and life, much like the odor of wet, warm earth reflecting summer thoughts. Wind brushed the trees, the tiny leaves of deciduous ones, and the pines with their needles sloughed gently in their tops. The adumbration of summer.

It was a magnificent morning just to be there seeing and sensing all this around. Two ducks, divers, skipped across the water and lifted into the air, wings rapidly beating, and after the water settled down, two geese glided over the house, making slight adjustments to their wings, and in formation, soared over the pines to the west and landed, the splashes making an echo in the river area. One loud honk escaped them as they settled onto the river.

Before they were out of sight, a kingfisher flashed over the water, on its way to dive after a minnow or perhaps returning. I have seen him flash the white underside of his body in a tight turn over the river before and watched as he dove ferociously into the water to capture a small fish. Usually, he then flew to a near branch and gulped down the fish or took it off to possibly a nest, to eat there, and perhaps feed his young, although this may be a bit early.

The vibrant smells of the north woods in spring are everywhere, the smell of earth, and pine, and wet wood rotting, and the slight sweet smell of tiny flower blooms. Later it will be strong. The trilliums are just beginning to blossom, and the forest floor will soon be filled with these lovely white and sometimes pinkish or bluish bugles that open so brightly and show their golden centers.

The air is carrying small feathery seed clusters from many trees, mostly the aspen, or popple as it is called here, and these light bundles of minute seeds float and fly along the woods and the river. The cove collects them and deposits them via the wind to the shore, where they line it futilely, at least for now.

Some of them, many of them, perhaps most, will land and germinate, and some will grow and be eaten or prevented in some way from growing, but many will grow, tall and rustling, and branched, and will become forest and part of the forest. Then they will spread seeds, year after year, until they crack and break or rot and finally fall to become part of the rich forest floor. Why? There must be some reason. Some creation plan for us to observe and think about these things is purpose in itself. To conclude the necessity of creation and Creator, and that these things are for man also, stems from these things, their existence, and our relationship to it.

The warming air pleases as it moves up the hill and over the trees and house and brushes the smell of the woods into a rich encompassing knowledge of the north woods.

A raven flies over the house to the river, and a big mallard drake, climbing fast along the pines over the river, silhouettes perfectly against the clouds as he turns to avoid the raven who, in an obvious majesty, beats slowly and regally down the river, the duck speeding past, beating rhythmically in the sunning spring air. The fluid silver/pewter of the clouds with thunder blue bases is the backdrop to this scene, and it is captured and stored in my brain and mind with countless others: the raven, wings regular, unruffled, the duck, active and aggressive flyer with the wings spread against the sky, the tops of pines just below it, the whole thing one in a second or two. A new scene will soon appear.

We were awakened a little after dawn by a sharp chirp or cluck sound, every five to ten seconds, from out in the yard. After listening a while I quietly left the bed and walked to the window. Not more than twenty-five feet away was a large tom turkey, wattle hanging down, strutting about in the yard, clucking regularly. He spread his tail feathers several times but never fully, and then, after a gobble or two, walked into the woods, perhaps not having attracted any females to the yard this time.

I have seen several turkeys in the area and their tracks on the road. This has been the closest to the house, and the birds, though not native to our area, have been doing fairly well during the last few mild winters. It will be a few years to decide if they can survive these northern winters.

After the recent rains and warming weather, everything in the woods begins to grow. The trilliums are developing, and the tips of the pines show their new tightly packed clusters of growth. In the yard on the east, shaded by very tall pines and spruce, three small delicate violets bloom, all alone and magnificently beautiful in their color against the green grass. They are like a centerpiece on a table or a fine painting hanging on the wall. The color of their violet is intense, like the color of most flowers, and draws the eye immediately. We wait to see if they will have partners. Their beauty is almost tangible. Even though they may not have partners, we will look at them often.

Sometimes when walking in the woods, one comes upon a cluster of flowers, or bushes, or trees that are beautiful in a special way. Alone and tucked into a corner of the woods where no one can see them, except by accident. How many lovely flowers and things remain hidden, yet they retain their beauty. It is like that with these violets.

This afternoon a large dark shadowy blue mass of clouds looms in the west, moving slowly toward us. It promises to be the first large thunderstorm of the year, and it is anticipated, although any storm, with its prodigious energy, is at the same time feared.

Against the expanding, rolling blue clouds an eagle silhouettes in a 90-degree bank, its white head, the sun gleaming off it, blazing in contrast.

The storm slowly moves on, the wind gentle and from the east, though the storm is coming from the west. A typical situation. The surface winds draw toward the storm that is sucking great amounts of air upward into itself.

But still the winds are mild, and the air warm and calm. The storm has a distance to go. Far off we hear a rumble of thunder, long and drawn out. We watch and wait, and even anticipate, but the storms are passing to the north, and we will not have the excitement of their nearness.

This afternoon I walked down to the cove and saw, while still some distance from it, a goose and a couple of small unusual looking ducks. Very slowly I walked toward them. The goose and its mate walked into the water, their long necks curved in a protective and aggressive show of defiance and defensiveness. When I reached the mowed open area by the cove I saw why. Swimming between the two guardian parents were four rather fuzzy-looking young goslings, clustered together obediently as they all swam toward the center of the river. They watched me as I watched them, and then I slowly walked back to the house hoping the goose family would return to the cove. Later, from the deck, I could see them strolling around the mowed area.

Today the clouds are rolling in again, sprinkling a gentle rain on the area, nipping the trees. Over the river the swallows are zooming in their great aerobatics in flying down insects. One swallow dives, flapping wings furiously, stiffens them and zooms upward in a soaring climb against the clouds, folds his wings and turns into another dive, wings extended.

Not only one but at least a dozen are feeding above the river. Some silently skim across the surface of the water in the evening when it is calm, catching insects either hatching or staying close to the water. These same low altitude flyers then will soar several hundred feet to feed at higher altitudes.

We're waiting for the nighthawks, those large pointed winged birds that zoom down in dives during mating season and make a roaring, booming sound. They are quite identifiable by the white spot on the wing and the bent shape of it. Like the swallows, the nighthawks are terrific aerobats, and zoom and climb and roll and turn and dive with the same facility as their cousins, the swallows and purple martins, except the nighthawks are much more powerful looking and more visible because of their size.

They perform wonderfully. It is not performance to them, of course. Perhaps it is to Him who ordered it. A part of the awesome narrative, and we should feel awe, for it stretches us and humbles us at the same time.

The clouds roll by, some dark budding thundershowers, lightly sprinkling rain on the woods and river, others simply undeveloped clouds passing along. The wind is mild, the woods silent except for the patter of occasional light showers. Perhaps a healthy thunderstorm will occur soon. Perhaps summer will come with a storm and mellow into its beauty, its ripe fullness coming after lightning and thunder and pelting rain.

Now, though, even the intermittent rain showers do not stop what must occur. The booming of male grouse continues through the woods, rolling in its rhythmic scale over one's ears. It is such an amazing deep sound, a throbbing call, a north woods call, a call of spring and mystery and wildness and warmth. To the grouse it is not such a thing. The grouse boom because they must. We listen because we find in it, in that sound, something to think about and relate to, something to wonder about. The grouse does not think about it or ask why. We must.

A robin has been standing in the backyard for the last half hour. So different from its usually busy and frenetic brothers and sisters, this one looks around, and straight up, and back, but does not move. Perhaps a young one, but not of this spring. It is too early yet. The robin may simply be resting. We will watch it. Fifteen minutes later the robin has flown away into the woods. Just flew away without explanation after confounding me with his stillness. Perhaps it really was just resting. Whatever the case, it was interesting to view the robin carefully. Perhaps it was posing.

The four goslings I saw yesterday have multiplied into nine. Today I saw the two Canada geese on the mowed cove area, and they shepherded nine little Canada geese, still looking fluffy and awkward, into the water. Of course, these could be a different pair since I have seen several pairs of Canadas along the river.

This evening the air is very calm, everything is very still, the river black, reflecting the birches across it. The smell of fresh cut lawn is heavy and pleasant, and the woods smells are pungent and good. God has given us the immeasurable even here.

The posing robin is back, back in the same spot he was in recently. He, or she, is again viewing the sky and the surroundings. There is obviously a possibility that this robin is simply a relative of the first one I saw passing, but it certainly would be a coincidence. This one stays about 15 minutes, in the same spot, then flies off. We will wait for him or her tomorrow.

A yellow shafted flicker, with its barred coat and part yellow tail and wing shafts, and the bright red, almost orange red spot on the back of its head, flew hard into the living room window. I found it upright, mouth open, shaken and dazed, below the window with some feathers plastered on it.

The bird simply stood, or rather, leaned on the ground, confused and obviously not in control. I moved it gently but it didn't respond. In the past I've found that it does take some time for them to recover from a heavy blow like this, so I left the flicker to watch it from inside.

By the time I was inside looking out, the injured flicker's mate, probably a male with its black bar to the side of the beak, the only apparent distinction in color between the male and female, had arrived, and facing its mate, began a series of bows and jerky head movements, culminating in its body and head pointed upward. I couldn't hear any sound, but it was moving its beak as though chirping.

The injured bird did not respond at first, but after a while began to turn its head and blink its eyes more quickly.

Soon its beak closed, and it looked a bit more normal. The mate continued its bowing action, occurring about every 20 seconds or so.

Finally, I went outside to see if my presence would galvanize the injured bird and cause it to fly. As I approached, the male flew off, and then seconds later the "shocked" flicker also flew off, maneuvered between branches, and landed high on a branch in a large pine. It appeared well as it flew away.

The actions of the male flicker appeared to indicate that a nest existed with eggs or young birds. Whatever the case, it was an interesting situation, without personifying the birds, and reflected a purpose and order that was being maintained. That drive for survival could not have simply been inherent in a purely cellular, biological sense. There was more complexity to it. A connection had been made. Not a logical one, but a signal had been received by the male bird. It had reacted probably because of its genetic makeup. However, it simply does not follow that this kind of function can stem from an early process that began with single-celled things unless there were some greater direction. Even the laws of thermodynamics indicate that complexity does not develop or evolve from the more simple. If we look at humans, the act of love for another in a human, the giving up of life for another, far exceeds the comparable support of animals, far exceeds the only main goal of a purely biological existence. The act of selfsacrifice, quite common in humans, in simple as well as in great acts, is contrary to and transcends the biological impulse of self-preservation.

The situation was an interesting one, and certainly a rare close look at another aspect of nature usually hidden to us.

The actions of the birds were terrific to observe. The parallel with humans adds many factors. For instance, the logical element leading to a conclusion to help another besides the instinctive aid of the physiological, the actual decision, based on free life, to stay and help in the face of possible injury or death, comes from the ability to conceptualize these elements and develop alternatives. And then, beyond all else, the idea of love is involved, love of the other, driven by an acceptance of God's continued love, and from that and because of it, love of God and commitment to God's law. The bird's act of support was different—stemming from God at another level.

Many differences, some similarities in the actions of animal and human, yet both point to something greater and beyond. To an initial, constant immensity, and to a final greatness. To find that greatness in contemplation is knowing inspired by love.

The morning is exceptionally clear, with a deep blue sky, an ocean blue sky, and the grass wet with dew and freshness. The smell of trilliums blooming in the woods is almost palpable. The delicate but tough white and bluish-tinged trilliums that now are appearing by the millions in the woods. Other flowers add their lovely scents to the wood smells, but they are still hidden.

The hummingbirds with their fantastic iridescent green backs and heads, and the males' almost glowing ruby throat are describable only in words still unreflective of their beauty. These tiny birds, delicate and long beaked, whirring wings and helicopterlike hovers, as well as strong and rapid flight, amaze and awe us. To be awed in the presence of beauty is especially ameliorative, pure and beyond salubrious.

We can sit below the feeder and soon the hummingbirds get used to us, fly about, and often hover several inches from our faces to get a better look, then dash away in their graceful swift flight, wings ablur. They also can jerk about, change direction almost in defiance of the laws of inertia, and suddenly stop, motionless in the air, their blur-fast wing beat holding them up. Sometimes one will sit and rest, and it looks so placid and tiny for a moment. Then suddenly it is energy again, pure activity in glow, green, white, and for the males, gleaming red throat.

The greens of the trees against that brilliant azure sky are also bright, almost glowing bright. Visibility must be excellent in these conditions, and the liveliness of everything seems to be heightened.

Today the hummingbirds reappeared. Two bright and aggressive ruby-throated hummingbirds jousted by the red vegetable-colored sugar and water "nectar" in the feeder.

These brilliant hovering arrows provide a zest and spice to everything in the area and pleasure for anyone watching.

SUMMER

THUNDERSTORMS ARE rolling along just to the north of us and to the southwest, the direction the back of the house and deck faces, and clouds are moving briskly in an otherwise mostly blue sunny sky. Some rain is gently falling while thunder roars to the north. Alongside the cove I am touched by the soft rain and watch the thunderstorms roar along over and beyond the house.

The breeze brings a smell of mint, fresh and springish, and then the odor enriches to swamp, a methany, pungent but familiar and good odor. Another rush of wind brings the smell of the cove. The wet smell is the breeze borne backdrop for the painting of smells, which in the summer includes the strong terebinthine scent of the pines, that identification of the woods so strong and so pleasant.

The sun is beginning to set in the clearing skies to the west, and the last of the thunderstorms passes far to the northeast. The water in the cove is very still as the wind calms and is also very clear. The smell now passes from afternoon to late spring evening, a moment of very delicate, sweet flower smell, another of swamp, then the mint, and underlying all, like the background on canvas, the wet smell of woods and grass and still the pine needles, the smell of river, the smell of clear air at the cove. These summer smells, developing now, are rich and deep.

The rain stopped this evening, and for a while, as the woods darkened, lightning bugs glowed their blinking lights in the woods, above which flashed refracted lightning from the storms some miles away. I stood on the deck watching the two kinds of light, the bugs flashing gently on and off, pinpoints in the woods, and the sky and clouds lighting up above, revealing curling shapes and billows. I stood watching until it was completely dark, and the drizzle turned to rain and drove me inside.

Later, after the rain had slowed to only a fine drizzle, the peepers began to sing again, and finally a few lightning bugs reappeared.

Off to the west lightning again began to flash, refracting in the clouds to form long glows above the horizon, golden shimmers in the clouds, almost like the quicker shining of the lightning bugs magnified and spread millions of times.

I went to bed with the sound of increasing rain pattering the roof, and quiet lightning glows occasionally touching the window.

Across the river this morning, the haze moved in and a gentle rain fell. Ducks and geese flew through it, a few peepers chirped, the deer came through the yard. We watched them with great enjoyment, watched them move through their environment, and ours. We watched them and saw order and beauty and grace, and from outside them, immutability. Conversing with nature while ignoring a cause, a Creator, is a one way conversation. Only the contemplative who opens soul to Creator receives the Word in a special clarity.

The rain still falls this evening and going to bed will be accompanied by the delicate roll of rain in timpani on the roof.

A tiny hopping creature on the road escapes my step and attracts my attention. The quarter inch long, ready to hop creature is a baby toad, frantically trying to get to the weeds and grasses on the other side. As I step slowly behind it, it becomes slower, exhausted, and rests a few feet from the edge. Finally, rested enough, it hops into the brush.

Down by the river the tiny baby blue eyes bloom along the water's edge, lovely dots of precise blue and gold and even a bit of white. Other flowers, in lesser numbers, accompany this crescendo of tiny colors.

These are many types of beauty. Yet perhaps the greatest beauty of nature I am aware of transcends the "environment" —that is my family and my relatives and my friends. Not always am I hospitable to them, my neighbors too, but despite that, the essence of awareness of the transcendental is there. The connection between baby toad and baby blue eyes is in one sense tenuous but real. The connection between family and friend, and indeed, neighbor, is real and natural, as well as purposeful. The connection is reality in the abstract, a soul "verbness" toward perfection in the Creator God.

By midafternoon the sky cleared and was dotted with fair weather cumulus, the puffy white clouds that sail briskly along in a clear blue sky, usually after a cold front passes. However, the brisk wind was moving another storm system toward us.

While looking over a pin cherry that the wind blew down in our yard, I noticed a bird rarely seen, or identified, up here. A turkey vulture or buzzard. At first I thought it was an eagle, but when it passed over the house, I couldn't see white tail or wings, and the wings were held at a strong V angle, definite indication of the buzzard. The eagle holds its wings more horizontally while soaring.

A few moments later in the back, while I sat on the deck, a male marsh hawk suddenly swooped down to the ground, then climbed and circled over the spot it had dived on. The hawk then turned into the woods, the tops of the trees hiding it, but in about 15 seconds reappeared, circling again over the "spot." There must have been a mouse or other rodent there that the hawk had missed. After some graceful circling, the marsh hawk finally flew off.

Within a few minutes of this interesting view, a hummingbird buzzed behind my head and then dashed to the feeder. It drank, backed off, searched the area for competitors, and shot off into the pines. I had been given a view of one of the largest birds in the area, the vulture, and the smallest, and in between, a look at a graceful and beautiful hunter, the hawk.

The rain is starting to fall now, not hard, yet not gentle, and I can see it strike the river and glint in the sunlight peeking barely between clouds. The smell of wet wood and rain and grass and a thousand ingredients comes to me on the burst of wind. Perhaps we will have a storm, for out west the clouds build, although I hear no thunder yet.

I walk through the rain this morning, clad in wet weather jacket and hood, the woods glistening, and my sneakers turning slowly darker with the rain. It is not a heavy rain, or a downpour, but a steady medium fall. The woods do look special, shining, with drops of rain falling from leaves and needle tips, paralleling the longer fall of drops from the clouds. Close to the mailbox, a scarlet tanager flashes across the road in front of me from the woods on the left to the woods on the right. But what a flash, a blaze of bright redorange with black wings. This is the first one we've seen here. Last year I spotted a few Baltimore orioles, but their color is distinctive. They too are brilliant, but the color is different, as is the placement of black on wings and head.

The rain sound is mesmerizing, soothing, and on the way back I stop often just to listen to it on the leaves. Also, I look for more scarlet tanagers, but see none, at least not today.

A glorious clear blue sky and a gentle wind send me down to the cove today after Mass. As I approach it, three ducklings splash and swim noisily out from the brush on the bank. They splatter through the bulrushes around the end of the cove. Soon they will be young ducks, more graceful, well formed.

Now they are gangly and clumsy looking, but capable of swift and judicious movement.

After their commotion died down, I could see thousands of minnows or small fish swimming in the shallows of the cove.

The sun shone clearly through the clear water onto the sandy bottom, spotlighting the minnows.

The river is running clear and bright, and the wind blows the smell of water and bulrushes and woods over to me as I walk slowly back to the house. The sun is warm on my back, the sky azure bright, the woods lush, and their shadows tremendous and mysterious and cool.

The coons came again this evening, two of them at the same time. They could have been siblings, twins even, so similar were they in size, shape, and markings. Coons, like other animals, do have differences if one studies them closely. These approached the bread and other scraps on the lawn below the deck, at twilight, and growled and snarled and chattered at each other, but approached no closer than about 10 feet. Every so often one of them would raise his (or her) head from the food, and arch its back and growl, whereupon the other would repeat the gesture. When they finished they each went on a scouting expedition of the yard, looking over their shoulders, and snarling or growling to serve notice.

As dark fell the coons strolled off into the woods, still suspicious of each other, but still together, and still appearing aloof, but wary of each other.

The stars appeared and multiplied, and the Milky Way, with the moon covered by clouds, appeared a swath of white, a natural pointillism, unbelievable numbers of stars and planets and whatever reflecting the sun's light or glowing on their own.

The immensity, the prodigious numbers, are simply awesome. Then, considering the actual size of these specks of light, the definition of universe comes to mind, and is almost too much to comprehend. Yet we are the only creatures that can comprehend the concept. And it is not the brain, the organ itself, the biological thing that conceptualizes universe or something like triangle. It is the intellect or soul, that separate essence, that something beyond, which can "think" of the concept of triangle without defining it with an image, which can understand what a triangle is, which can "see" the universe without ever having seen the universe. Universality is the domain of the "intellect," soul, particularity, imagination, mind.

When we look up at the stars, they can be spots, as they appear to the brain, or planets, stars, things, as they are learned, conceptualized by the intellect, and part of the vastness yet connectedness and order of the universe.

Those other bright spots, the fireflies, or lightning bugs as we called them when we grew up in the city, are flickering and glowing in the woods, always a mysterious yet pleasant and anticipative activity. They are close and familiar, familiar in a different way than the stars, which flicker coldly and sharply (depending on our mood) or change to warm embracing brightness. The lightning bugs are constant and glow periodically in their movement through the dark. Their fire does not burn, nor does it light too well, but it is familiar and brighter than the dark of the nighttime woods.

The clouds, large cumulus, and the broader covering alto stratus, rolled in at twilight covering the stars. A coon came by this early evening after a hot, muggy day, and stood below the house, stretching to see me standing behind the kitchen window. It stood on its hind legs, stretching its head. Finally, after weaving from side to side, the coon dropped to all fours and unconcernedly strolled into the woods.

To the southwest, lightning flashed over the sky, and after a long time a low rumble echoed over the river. There was not a breeze, not a movement of air here on the deck, but the clouds sailed across the sky, and the lightning flashes glowed over the billows and curls of thunder clouds. Near the river frogs croaked and pinged, not the peepers, who have been silent since they laid their eggs a few weeks ago, but other frogs that live in and near the river. Occasionally, a bull frog twanged like the deepest note of a bass violin. The lightning bugs flickered silently, changing positions constantly among the trees, even toward the tops of pines and spruces east of the house that stretch 70 feet, and whose silhouettes stand etched against the sky slightly lighted by refraction from the city five miles away.

To the southwest the storm closes, the lightning visible as streaks between ground and sky and cloud to cloud, the roar and burst of thunder constant. This storm will miss us to the south but will provide a marvelous spectacle, always a new and inspiring experience.

I watched the grandiose display, rich and varied and explosive and unstoppable, rolling across the sky until a few rain drops fell, and I felt sleepy. The storm receded, visibly distant, auditorially fading, and the rain drops slowing their plinking and splatting on the deck.

The lightning bugs still blinked quietly in the trees and the wind began to blow gently. The frogs still sang their slow pianissimo chorus. Things rustled in the woods, the thunder turned into a dim throaty rumble, and finally turned into a mellow soft vibrato fade.

The thunder fades, but the distant hoot of an owl separates the silence, the soft, distant hoot again. The owl is hunting, like most of the nighttime predators.

The predator-prey relationship is natural. It reflects a certain order. Yet the question of suffering is mysterious. In human nature, bare, raw human nature, unproscribed by value and law and self-discipline, there is also suffering. There is suffering of all kinds in every human's life, no matter the level of civilization. There is the biological plane of self- survival. Beyond that, however, are those elements that transcend the purely biological. Those elements that predicate values, and laws, and self-discipline, those that rise above and beyond the pathological. Human nature is that barest, atavistic drive, amalgamated in a marvelous way with the highest drive, those elements of free will as opposed to intuitive existence, conceptualization rather than simply imagination, and the awareness of intellect and conscience, that quality which discerns and distinguishes values in acts. Yet we all suffer at one level or another. That can be offered to the ineffable incarnate Word, Christ.

The soul paints all around with the body. The body's alleged final fall only impedes an element. Christians know it will return, and the teachings of Christ reflect a view, a Creator's view, that nothing is created to be dispatched to nothingness. That which goes to nothingness chooses nothingness itself. The canvas will be completed. Thus, it is good to remember that the chipmunk, or wolf, or hawk, or rabbit can do no inherent wrong. Humans, of course, can by acceptance of wrong, by ignoring that which they, and not the animals, have. There are questions of justice and charity there also, as well as faith and hope. The sense of the world as only material is a disordered one.

The night is so far along now even the fireflies have limited their display, even the stars are hazy from the clouds creeping in on silent steps.

If all the philosophers who have ever lived were here, how would we listen to them?

All the great saints? Perhaps the conclusion is that it really is prayer that is the most important thing in the world. There are many important things, prayer chief among them. Prayer, union with God, contemplation. That's where Christ tells us to start. It may take us lifetimes to see that. There are so many mysteries, so many wonderful things, so few answers, yet only a very few are necessary and one most important.

It is very hot now, in the eighties in early evening, but there is shade on the house and deck from the pines and cedars to the west. The summers here are short but rich and beautiful and full and ripe. Spring and fall are usually short, and so clearly transitional, but winter bites, and holds on, but it too has beauty. The summers, though, are magnificent.

On the deck, while watching the river, I heard a scratching sound from below and saw a medium-sized raccoon climbing onto the deck from the support post beneath. The coon saw me, but I moved to the patio door and went inside. It waited for a moment, then examined every corner of the deck. Finally, it lay down, mouth open, panting, obviously hot.

It stretched out its head to lie flat on the deck, its hind legs out to either side, the ringed fluffy tail between, and the front paws on either side of its head.

After resting this way a few minutes, it yawned, got up, and strolled to the window from which my daughter and I watched. The coon was a female, probably with young somewhere, for her nipples and extended breasts were visible. She appeared quite young, though, and this may have been her first birthing.

She kept rising on her hind legs in order to look into our window, and we finally walked slowly to the screen patio door. The coon joined us, on the outside, as we watched each other, my daughter speaking gently to the coon, and the coon watching curiously. Then it walked close to the screen and lay down, again its head stretched out on its chin, like a tired cat or dog.

We wondered if this raccoon had ever been someone's pet, it was so casual near humans. It stayed around for about an hour and a half and then, no doubt urged by motherhood or some other call, climbed down the deck and disappeared into the darkening woods. An altogether unusual and interesting experience.

"Connie" or "Ms. Coon," as my daughter and I respectively called the visiting raccoon, is a "Mrs." after a fashion. She brought her four young babies with her tonight. They lined up on the deck railing and watched, chattering continually, while I fed Connie by hand, admittedly not a wise thing to do with a wild animal. I consoled myself by remembering that my hand was only a few inches beyond the screen door. I won't do it again, though, simply because we don't want the coon, and her babies, to be too complacent near humans, some of whom, in their excitement, may take a shot at a coon simply for the adventure of it. Or something.

Down by the cove, tall Angelica are blooming, their white flowers clustered like saucers. They are about four to five feet tall and stand out above the weeds. Also, the beautiful "blue flags," an iris family flower, are blooming among the weeds by the cove.

The baby geese of a few weeks ago are now flying, still not perfectly, but able to move well. Two of them were surprised by me at the cove this afternoon and immediately took off, running on the water and beating their long and growing wings heartily, although still somewhat clumsily. Within the clumsiness, though, was visible strength and coordination and smoothness.

A muskrat swam by, and I stood very still so it wouldn't notice, and it swam across the cove gently and casually, disappearing in the bulrushes.

On the way back to the house I saw several king-birds, or perhaps they were phoebes, the first I've noticed this summer, hovering over the weeds to catch insects. These handsome birds have a nest nearby, I'm sure, for they stayed in the area below the house until dark covered them.

At the house the woodchuck, which I hadn't seen for a month or so, appeared on my woodpile. It is a sleek and good looking chuck. When I stopped it stopped also, but I won the patience contest because after a few minutes it ducked quickly among the logs in the woodpile. I'm not so sure now I won the patience contest.

This beauty here is overwhelming at times, so many things to admire and see, and sometimes sorrow for. Yet the beauty here extends beyond when people are present too. Solitude is necessary, and some find it more important than others. Still, contact with people is even more necessary, and fulfillment lies in union with God reflected by our relationships with others, and with the rest of God's creation. But occasional solitude allows us to hear better, and to see better, and ultimately to be able to listen, to contemplate, and thus know the truth better, know God better.

Beauty, however we describe it, exists because we need to see beauty, be aware of it through our senses, in order to perceive the source, in order to be aware of it in God, the ultimate of all beauty. At least at first, we need the elements of beauty, which are really abstract.

So Christ, the incarnate word of God, exists, the full connection of the world and beauty. We are incapable of understanding on our own the nonincarnate, the abstractly perfect transcendent God of beauty. Christ the incarnation of God's word reaches us as a bridge, a hand pulling us above the nothing, to God, the Creator of everything, the ultimate. Perhaps an instant of awe at a flower, or drop of dew, or storm, or rainbow, or animal, or other man or woman, or friend, or family, or thought, or love, or action in God's awareness is that ineluctable gift of beauty given to us to see for ourselves what possibilities transcend us. "Contemplation does not rest until it has found the object that dazzles it," says Josef Pieper.

The sun is setting beyond the trees, and the hill down to the river, completely covered with white and blue bush clover, is in shadow. The tiny marsh-fox grow here too, mixed in with the other more obvious brush cloves.

Connie and her coon babies are visible waddling slowly toward the woods, Connie looking back at the house, perhaps to see if we have more food. They continue, a retinue of secret creatures seen by us, a gift to us this summer, preceded by and followed by greater gifts, all bundling and connected in the convolution and amalgamation of a gift of beauty.

A great blue heron rows away, long thin legs trailing water from its takeoff in the bulrushes. The water is calm on the river, and in the shallows and the cove the heron hunts silently, well camouflaged, moving so slowly it blends into the vertical water plants. It flies almost ponderously, but there is little need for quick maneuvering for this bird.

The sun is setting and the house is in the shadow of the tall pines and spruces on the west side. The air is almost perfectly calm with an occasional touch of breeze. In the backyard chipmunks hop jauntily from one side to the other, their tails held vertically like car antennae or markers. They are very active, although one often sees a chipmunk sitting on a rock "clucking," its eyes almost closed, just making the "cluck" sound regularly, its tail jerking at every sound.

They look well fed now as we approach midsummer. The weeds and grasses are thick, and seeds and insects plentiful.

The deer are, as usual, plentiful also. We saw our first fawn of this year just recently, spots thick on its sides. There may also have been a twin. We'll probably find out soon, as they will be around the big oaks in our yard when they begin to drop acorns.

This morning at about four I awoke and lay surprised that I was awake until I heard a noise outside. That is what awakened me. It was the howling of coyotes and was surprisingly close. I could make out three distinct parts to the harmony, at least. The sound moved close, and in a few minutes evolved into a yapping and singing like a playful tune.

I climbed out of bed and squatted by the long window, cranking it open more. The yapping continued, a cross between a short howl and yelp, not a bark at all. Soon the sound was very close, at the edge of the front yard by the driveway, and I could see shadows moving about.

The yapping would continue for a while, the shadowy coyotes jumping about and playing, and then turn into that melodious high-pitched howl that so epitomizes the wilderness, both here in the north and in the west.

I sat, fully absorbed for several minutes, then woke my wife. She listened also as finally the coyotes moved down the driveway and into the woods still yapping playfully and interspersing their short calls with long clear howls, the second and third voices joining after the pauses. Silence returned as I strained my ears for more. They had gone. And I looked forward to hearing them again. Those clever, tough singers in the woods.

I thought of Ernest Thompson Seton's books that I had read as a boy, and his friendly stories of the coyote, a symbol of the west, and really, of the north now too and the whole country, since most of the wolves are gone.

I will listen for the coyotes again, listen for their eerie and wonderful harmony, listen for their interesting and rich melody, listen to the woods and hear other secrets being told. Once in a great while the sound of a wolf rolls along the air, deep and decidedly different from a coyote's howl. There are not many left in this part of the country, but I have seen, several times, on the sandy part of the driveway, which I rake regularly to capture footprints left at night, the broad, large prints of a wolf, and more often, but not regularly, heard the bass howl of the wolf, a wilderness song certainly. My brother and I have seen a wolf once in the woods, and fairly close. We both looked each other over, and it walked slowly away into the bush, with a parting glance back over its shoulder. We watched it walk away until it disappeared.

Early today, when the risen sun's shadows stretched the woods, a fawn, spotted over its body, walked nervously across the front yard, aiming toward the coughing calls of its mother. Delicate and graceful, it stopped often, ears upright and turning, until it stepped carefully into the woods to the side of the house. This is the youngest one I've seen in the yard this summer.

Later in the afternoon, a very warm summer day with cumulus building to the southwest, I saw a great variety of birds. From the deck and the driveway I saw a vulture, soaring without moving a wing, for over three minutes, and riding the same thermal with it, two large hawks, dwarfed by the vulture, but, probably from their silhouette, red-tailed hawks. Soon after these disappeared to the east, a small bird lashed furiously at a crow, which tried vainly to dodge the small bird's vicious attacks. The crow called wildly and almost yelped every time the small bird struck the crow's head.

Later, on the deck, watching the storm build to the southwest, I saw a great blue heron flying away from the storm, several ducks flashing low across the river, a few blue jays feeding in the yard, a lone night hawk flying very high and being blown eastward by the wind, several flights of small birds that I was unable to identify, and the omnipresent hummingbirds, buzzing over my head at the feeder. The rain is falling as I write this and lightning flashes across the blue gray clouds. The backyard slope to the river is filled with bluish and white brush clover plants and they are bright and glowing in the fresh rain. The river is a sheet of wrinkles and splashes from the rain, and even the dragonflies, visitors around the deck every summer day, are gone. Best of all gone are the black flies, who, before a coming storm, my mother often said, will bite ferociously. They did.

It is not difficult to accommodate a negative like that with everything else we've been given. Especially today, the feast of Our Lady of Mount Carmel.

This evening after the storms the breath of flowers came over the river. Perhaps it was the flowers on our slope to the river, but I doubt it. The fragrance existed even on the driveway, the end of it, and everywhere. Even the harsh odor of skunk, which lasted a few seconds on the wind, dissipated, and the flowers' welcome filled the air in the twilight.

Connie (the raccoon) is visiting in the evenings regularly and sometimes brings her five, not four, babies. They have grown quickly and now fight over food, attack their mother's tail, and run about and play. They are simply fun to watch. She has stopped coming onto the deck since we stopped putting food there, and it is better for her not to become too casual around humans.

The past week the weather has been hot and muggy. Rain showers and occasional thunderstorms, and great cloud formations. Tonight the rain fell, and now it is warm and humid, the dark clouds floating somnolently past, barely moving, and the frogs beginning to croak down by the river. The air is very still and the black flies vicious down by the river, particularly in the brush with no wind.

The bats are beginning to flash across the sky in their peculiar but efficient angular way, angular because of the silhouette they present with their joints at the front of the wing.

By the cove the leopard frogs leap in green rainbow arcs out of the mowed grass into the deep and thick weeds. The river is flat calm and black, reflecting the dark clouds above.

In the woods the rustles of leaves and twigs signal quiet life and death. The night is falling, has fallen imperceptibly over the woods.

These are the hot days of summer. Humid often, with billowy huge cumulus clouds developing into cumulonimbus that bring heavy rain showers and lightning and sometimes hail. These are the barefoot days, and shirtless days, but of course, one is wise to keep the insects at bay. The mosquitoes and black flies, midges, ticks, and other creatures that, despite their existence and function in a plan, are somewhat pesty. Of course, we really don't know everything, so it is necessary to bear with them.

These warm days see a lush growth of flowers and trees and grasses as well as the rapid maturation of the young animals. Everything prepares for the fall and winter, the dormant period. But now, it is pleasant to enjoy the warmth and fragrant breezes and thunderstorms, the foggy cool of morning already with its hint of heat, the burning midday sun, the breathless twilight, and the nighttime stars or lightning flashes on the horizon.

These days are special, as are all those given us, but these are gift special summer days.

A magnificent morning, cool, with fog lying on the river and wrapped around the trees along the shore. The ridge one mile to the southeast is barely visible with the tendrils of fog floating about gently. The sky above is clear blue, and when the sun rises, clearing away the fog and the cold dew on the grass, it will be warm. The spider webs in the meadow are etched with dew, looking like geometrically designed glass filaments, pure silver shine in designs defying simple description, yet which are simplicity themselves. Every web features the geometry of the natural law, never varying from those principles, and yet every one innovative in countless degrees and combinations. It can be described scientifically. It would only, however, be the description of accidentals and can truly only be described as essence with its accidentals. Described fully perhaps only as poem, it cannot just mean, but must be. It is not just vector angles and forces, it is beauty, truth, and value, those inseparable abstractables.

Soon after dawn this morning a presentation of sounds began. Off in the distance thunder rolled, and then we heard crows calling and coming closer. The rain began to patter on the roof and then, with thunder increasing, the rain roared down. Two blue jays began to call to each other in the yard, and several other birds began to call as the first burst of rain slowed.

The thunder rolled, and the crows called farther away, the jays kept calling to each other, still in the yard. The rain drummed the roof and the thunder pounded counter-point over the sharp sounds of jays and the staccato crow calls. Behind this aural display the other birds, chirping and singing, wrens and chickadees, called rather happily. As the daylight increased, the storm moved on. The woods returned to the daily sounds, covered by the breaking clouds and bluing sky.

Against an almost white blue glaring sky in the southwest, with the sun setting, five ducks flew rapidly out of the sunset, over the trees by the river, and dove in unison toward the water, where they disappeared below the trees and brush along the river. The breeze is cooling after a very warm and beautiful day, the air clear and the wind enough to keep the heat from being oppressive.

The evening cool is upon us now and the occasional breeze blows through the house, refreshingly pleasant. Outside we can hear Connie the coon chuckling and whirring, her sounds to the young coons, although we've only seen her feeding alone in the yard recently. The young may have become mature enough to go off just a bit on their own some of the time, although they still run to her often enough.

The young birds are flying with the adults now, and only rarely do we see a very young looking bird hopping after its mother on the lawn in front of the house.

Over the river the young geese have taken to working their wings in low flights up and downstream. There are from two to three to as many as twenty, evidently preparing, in their way, for the long trip south in the fall.

The fawns are active and rather aggressive, bolting from their mother and leaping about, running in circles, chasing each other. Soon they will begin to lose their spots.

This time of summer is a maturing time for most animals and plants, and the woods are thick, heavy with foliage, and the grasses tall. Soon the seeds too will mature and feed the animals that eat them, and feed the earth to grow into new plants, and feed into beauty in their own way. St. Augustine comments that the world is subject to change. The Creator is not subject to change. His beauty is constant and eternal.

New flowers spring up regularly, though, and we have clusters of blue and purple thistle flowers blooming, and blue phlox, with their rich perfume, clustering along the trail to the river. The scent of flowers is rich on the trail and down by the river, especially in the morning calm and again in the evening.

Summer itself is also maturing this time of year, and pouring out its beauty everywhere.

The remains of a small deer along the blacktop road off our driveway are attracting many animals that eat carrion or freshly killed game. It has been eaten so much that the rib cage is exposed, and today I saw closely two of the great "cleansers" of the wilderness areas, the turkey vulture and its very close cousin, the black vulture.

As I drove past the carcass of the deer and flushed several crows, a shadow, large and broad winged crossed the hood of the car. At first I thought an eagle had caused it, but looking back, I saw a large dark bird, with no white on it, settle into a tree above the deer carcass. Not far away, in another pine, sat a black vulture. I backed up the car and got within 30 feet of a large turkey vulture that, upon my leaving slowly, leaped gently down to its meal.

Within a few days the deer remains will be totally gone, and there will be no reminder at all that the creature died and "disappeared" at that spot. Yet we know that all creation will be renewed.

The last week has been very hot and humid, particularly in this part of the north woods. The temperature has hovered around 85-90 degrees and the humidity has been high. The breeze kept things rather pleasant, but on days when it was calm, even the trees wilted under the heat.

It was certainly August summer weather, and the deer kept to the dense shady areas for a few days until it cooled again.

This morning the rain roared down, pounding the roof and lashing the leaves. It cooled but has remained humid. There will be more hot weather this summer, but after this rain a cool high pressure area should move in for a few days. For at least a while we will have pleasant cool weather, but all weather is really pleasant if accepted in the right way. There are advantages to the changing weather much of the country has.

The hummingbirds were jousting around the feeder this morning, and the dominant one was extremely busy chasing and forcing off the others that were trying to feed. Eventually, he chased one far enough away so others could feed, but he returned, and sat imperiously on the beam from which the feeder hangs, even in a rain like now. At one point four hummingbirds were circling and shooting about, trying to gain an advantageous position for feeding. The rain has not stopped them, except during its heaviest falls.

A curious confrontation occurred last night in the backyard.

About 10 pm a handsome skunk strolled into the yard and began to eat some scraps we left for Connie and her youngsters.

The skunk was placidly eating the snacks when Connie appeared with her five babies (which are now about half Connie's size), and walked directly to some food a few feet from the skunk and began to eat. The skunk moved back, raised its tail, and we thought it would spray the area and Connie. It only snarled a bit and rushed at Connie, who snatched a bit of food and walked, quickly, off a few feet. The skunk resumed its meal also.

This interlude was quickly broken when one of the young coons, which were in a circle about 10 feet from the skunk, aggressively approached the food and began to eat. The skunk stepped back, then rushed at the coon, snapping its jaws at the young one. The little coon, obviously having attained some natural wisdom, leaped away and returned to the circle of its siblings.

This action lasted another half hour, the young coons being driven off every time they approached the food, and the skunk becoming aggressive in defending its "stock." At one point three small coons were attempting to snatch food and the skunk obviously had had enough of the exasperation and released its odiferous weapon. The little coons ran out to their circle, but Connie, an experienced mother, shook her head and returned for more food. The skunk threatened her, and she strolled away with a bit of it, while the skunk finally settled down to finish eating.

After reviewing this interesting conflict, we realized that everyone involved had eaten something, due to the skunk's apparent civility, or more likely, mild nature. The skunk only released its gas attack when it seemed to be personally threatened, and neither Connie nor the babies attempted to attack the skunk. Later the skunk, a victor of sorts, strolled into the woods, at least 10 minutes after Connie and the young coons left, departing the aromatic scene of its encounter.

The hot, humid summer continues, interspersed with cooling thunderstorms. Today during the walk on the drive I found a small grass snake and carried it into the mowed grass. It wiggled away furiously into the tall grass next to the yard.

Also, while retrieving the paper from the box, I noticed a large spider on it, unusual for its color, which was a very light beige. Perhaps they are common, but obviously difficult to see. As menacing as a spider can look, its color was quite striking.

On the way back I ate wild raspberries that line the driveway on both sides most of its length. Almost every walk we take this time of year is interspersed by snacks of juicy, and very tasty, raspberries. The bears will be about to have some soon, also, so we compete, in a way, with them to eat raspberries.

The summer is rich and full and pleasant, filled with ripe odors and scents of the woods and flowers, and with wonderful fruits, both edible and abstract.

All creatures enjoy it, in some way, because they exist in it. We enjoy it and know we enjoy it. We create the cathedral in all its architectural magnificence to concentrate our awareness of our environment and ourselves to that which transcends us. Our awareness of the great and deep beauty and complexity of nature is joined to our question of "why," and our own intellectual awareness of it provides answers.

Nature around us is quite incomplete without the creature of mankind, with the ability to conceptualize and choose. Even with suffering, like much of what mankind endures, there is the gift of life and love, the act of dying for and before the other, with the ability to see right and wrong, with the awareness of dignity, awareness of God. We read that God did not stop at nature but continued, creating us. And we can perceive the beauty of it and God. Nature is, as Malcolm Muggeridge points out, "Parable."

The ineffable Word also comes to us in Eucharist. The host of simple, common wheat, and wine from grape, the most natural elements, become, as Christ told us, the Glorified Christ, the ultimate gift among all the gifts we have been given in superabundant, unconditional love.

Another summer day, another gift, begins with a doe and fawn feeding in the yard. The sky is clear, clean blue, and the smell of luxuriant summer wood dampness wafts across the yard.

All day the southwesterly breezes blow and the skies stay clear, with occasional cumulus puffs. The afternoon is the sound of warm wind soughing in the tall pines by the house, and the scent of pine needles that carpet the ground beneath them.

The river is wrinkled with wind and sparks the reflection of sunlight with every gust. Warm ground, and soft grass, and the warmth of August are here, in the bending tips of trees and rustling leaves, the scents of pines and flowers, the smell of wood and earth and river.

The connection between the rest of nature and mankind is great, as is the transcendence of soul to all other mutable nature. It is all part of God's creation. The abstract elements are lasting; the mutable, by definition, are not, in one form. These are combined to make a special beauty which we seek, and they relate their story, their narrative, their parable to us if we open ourselves to listen, and we open ourselves to the Creator, who tells us in inimitable ways what is true. These combinations we search for in the beauty all around us must lead us to a greater beauty if it is not to be simply superficial, if it is not to end in some dreary nothingness contrary to those drives of the spirit.

The contemplative Adrienne von Speyr relates that "one can get some notion of the infinite multiplicity of relations in God by contemplating the world: if the world's variety is so colorful, fascinating, exciting and inexhaustible, how rich must the source of this variety be."

This afternoon we walked through the woods west of the house toward the river. The woods here are thick with balsam and cedar and are dark, the tall pines and balsams shading everything from the sun. And the deciduous trees in almost full color, not quite reaching the apogee of brightness, but vividly colorful, especially in the sun, contrast with the greens of balsam and pine and cedar, lending the whole area and its inhabitants an almost surrealistically beautiful stage.

The slope to the river here is steep, though colorful and vibrant, and we were hot and perspiring freely when we came to a clearing by the river. My wife saw them first. Four ruffed grouse sitting quietly in some brush on the river bank, no more than 30 feet from us. I walked closer and they didn't move. I stepped to within 10 feet of them and they sat quite still, only their heads moving slightly. After watching a while, I moved away, surprised at the lack of vigilance of these birds. Usually they would have flushed noisily, but for some reason they didn't. On the way back to the house on our path from the cove, where we eventually arrived, two grouse flushed loudly from the pines on the east. They were at least 50 feet away from us when they rose. No research will explain that difference.

The woodchuck is back in our front yard, very alert, nibbling some kind of weeds or grasses. It rushes off to the woods at the slightest sound. It is very alert and fat. It should have a good winter's sleep the way it looks.

Tonight is calm and still after last night's violent thunderstorms and yesterday's rains. The river is exceptionally calm, reflecting the woods in perfect stillness on the other side and the blue and gray clouds against the pink/magenta setting sun sky.

A few ripples occur on the surface of the mirror water from rising fish and three large splashes of a fairly large fish jumping. I think they may be largemouth bass, by the location and the sound, one at least big enough to make a large splash. Of course, it could have been a northern pike or even a small to medium musky.

Before the ripples settle from the jumping fish a great blue heron flies down river past the cove, its reflection just inches below it, perfectly matching the slow graceful beats of its broad powerful wings. The heron settles gently in shallow water across the river and stands motionless, a curve of blue gray against the darkening reeds and woods.

Night is coming in a long, settled, lovely calm here on the river by the cove.

These last few days have been the prerequisite and ultimate in early fall. Mild during the day, cool at night with intermittent days of showers and very gentle rain.

The leaves are just beginning to turn on some maples, and more birch are showing yellow and brownish tinges. Across the river is a toning, a hint of reds in the maples behind the birch. The rich greens are turning to the deep wild variety of color of the autumn season.

Last night, very clear and cool, the stars cold bright, a group of coyotes went singing. I awoke to the clean and mellow howl of one coyote, soon joined by another, and finally ended up hearing a series of yelps and yapping, as though they were partying and laughing.

The calls lasted a few more minutes and then silence. The coyotes moved away, leaving me hoping I'd hear them again soon.

The morning broke clear and cool, dew painting the grass and weeds, and if you looked toward the rising sun in the east, you would see hundreds of small spider webs in the field below the house. Hundreds of little webs trapping the dew and glistening, reflecting the rising sun. One field of sparkling jewels. They will soon break down from the wind, but will probably be there tomorrow morning if it doesn't rain.

The clouds are moving in slowly from the west. A low bank, slowly rolling in. It will be a quiet pre-autumn rain.

Today is an Indian Summer day, warm and clear with a gentle fresh breeze. The trees are beginning to turn colors more now. The display is beginning in earnest. The woods are becoming variegated with the hint of fall, the diversity and depth of color cheering and awesome. The hummingbirds are gone, having heeded the call to fly south, having flown in the last week or so.

Yesterday, a large flock of Canada geese was forming into a V and returning south.

Walking on the drive today I spotted a garter snake sunning itself on the gravel road. It had a definite lump in the middle and was not a "slender fellow" as was Emily Dickinson's. This snake had evidently just eaten a small frog or toad or other small animal and was snoozing. I walked up to it and had to prod it to get it to move off the road. A handsome snake, green striped with orange and white parallel stripes. We, as children, called them "grass" snakes. They are usually identified as "garter" snakes, and eat large amounts of insects and some small rodents.

The last several days during my walks in midafternoon I have heard a booming grouse. Always from the same area. It can't be mating, since that season for grouse passed in the late spring. It could be simply a territorial warning that occurs whenever I pass close to that area on the road. It is a curious situation and rather interesting.

Today an encounter with another grouse. On my way to the cove, walking softly with the gentle breeze in my face, I heard a gentle chucking. Recognizing it might be a grouse, I slowed down and looked around under the branches of the balsam fir to my left, off trail. There was a grouse, tail fanned out fully, neck ruffs spread handsomely, dancing about and clucking softly. There were no other grouse nearby, at least visible, and the dancer slowly moved deeper into the brush while I watched from no more than 15 feet away. Perhaps there was a mate nearby, hidden from view. However, this time of year is not mating time. The grouse may simply have been going through some formal routine. We don't know everything about life, even animal life, so it may have been some activity very normal to a grouse at this time.

While I stood watching, a chickadee flew to a twig a few feet from my face and chirped pleasantly. That reminded me again of the lovely flights of migratory birds that soon will fill the sky. The passage of season paralleled by the passage of birds from one zone to another, really one passage causing another. And so it is that one must, in the overflow at least of all the gifts given us, graciously and humbly thank God, Love and First

Cause, for only great and abiding love can give us all we have and ultimately give us ourselves, our life.

Early this morning, a windy gray rainy day, out on the deck, I found a large bird sitting in a huddled position, looking rather stunned. It had apparently flown into a window. There were no feathers or marks on the windows, so I surmised the bird would survive.

It was a kingfisher, that regal looking gray-blue bird with white crest and collar and barred tail, which dives into the water for small fish. This one was a female, with a chestnut colored band across the lower breast. They were often near the house, moving through the woods and over the river. The kingfisher has a marvelous blue crest on its head, and I was able to caress this one gently, while it still was dazed, its long beak slowly opening and closing.

I gave it a bowl of water and after a short while the bird dipped its beak into it. It became more alert gradually and finally began to look around. I approached it again and caressed its back gently, and after a few seconds it simply leaped into the air and flew away, strong wing-beats carrying it around the house.

This was a rare opportunity to see the kingfisher up close, since they are rather wary, and few wild birds, other perhaps than the chickadee, are tame or fearless enough to be approached very closely.

By the time the kingfisher flew off, the mist that swaddled the river and the trees began to slacken and some blue parts began to show in the sky. The wind continued, showering clusters of leaves from the trees across the river where they fell onto the water and were borne away. The heavy gusts blew batches of needles from the pines and they looked like sleet roaring down. The real sleet will be coming soon.

In the afternoon, as I walked down the road, now open to bright, warm sunlight, I heard an unusual clattering noise. I stopped and saw, about 50 feet away, a whitetail buck rattling his antlers, about four points, against a pile of cut down branches. At times the bucks have boldly walked into our yard and rubbed their antlers against the trees, wearing off much of the bark. They will also attack brush piles or bushes, in fact, almost anything to bang their antlers against.

I banged my walking stick against a similar pile of brush by the road, and the buck straightened its head and glared in my direction. It appeared highly disturbed by my commotion, and, as soon as it had ascertained I was human rather than a challenging buck or accommodating doe, bolted into the brush, the white underside of its tail flashing left and right.

Summer is almost over. The magnificence of it is beginning to change to a different beauty, the season is moving on. Every season is one for contemplation: of nature, of God, of the richness of summer, with its fullness of gifts, easing into another season not with a whimper or a bang but in an almost esoteric silence, especially fitting, whatever the time, for contemplation.

So "Let all the earth cry out with joy to the Lord."

www.ingramcontent.com/pod-product-compliance
Lightning Source LLC
Chambersburg PA
CBHW021833020426
42334CB00014B/604

* 9 7 8 0 9 8 2 9 9 0 4 0 7 *